RENEWALS 458-4574

DATE DUE

GAYLORD			PRINTED IN U.S.A

KAIZEN TEIAN 2

Guiding Continuous Improvement Through Employee Suggestions

Edited by the Japan Human Relations Association

Foreword by
Linda Topolsky

Publisher's Message by
Norman Bodek

Productivity Press
Portland, Oregon

Originally published by Nikkan Kogyo Shimbun, Ltd., Tokyo. Copyright © 1990 Nikkan Kogyo Shimbun, Ltd. Translated into English by Productivity Press. Translated by Steve Vitek.

Edited by the Japan Human Relations Association
Text by Bunji Tozawa, Managing Editor, JHRA
Illustrations and cartoons by Misako Fukui and Mio Asahi

Productivity Press
P.O. Box 13390
Portland, OR 97213-0390
Telephone: (503) 235-0600
Telefax: (503) 235-0909
E-mail: service@ppress.com

Cover design by Joyce C. Weston
Printed and bound by Edwards Brothers
Printed in the United States of America

Library of Congress Cataloging-in-Publication Data

Kaizen teian. 2. English.
    Guiding continuous improvement through employee suggestions = Kaizen teian 2 / edited by the Japan Human Relations Association.
        p. cm.
    Includes index.
    ISBN 1-56327-188-5
    1. Problem solving. 2. Suggestion systems. I. Nihon HR Kyōkai.
II. Title. III. Title: Guiding continuous improvement through employee suggestions.
HD30.29.K44 1992
658.4'03—dc20   91-46259
                                                                            CIP

First paperback edition 1997

02 01 00 99 98 97   12 11 10 9 8 7 6

Contents

Publisher's Message

What do you think of when you think of employee involvement? Every day, millions of people arrive on the job at factories, offices, and shops. They do their jobs and work hard at them — but involvement is not the same as "working hard." In too many cases, it is as if there were signs posted over the entrances of our workplaces that read, "Stifle intelligence upon entering." Workers are seen as expendable resources brought in to do the required tasks; rarely are they asked to use their brains to improve the work.

Involvement really represents a new dimension in working. People are truly involved only when they have a creative contribution to make in doing their work and in finding ways to do it better. The job itself may bring us the physical security and sense of social belonging that Maslow documented as among our basic needs. To fulfill our higher needs for recognition and self-development, however, each of us needs opportunities to share our creativity and intelligence.

A participative suggestion system is an excellent method for providing creative opportunities on a daily basis. The first volume in this series, *Kaizen Teian 1*, described in detail the reasons for using such a system to build involvement, making the case for it as a means of managing improvement and offering practical insight into how to administer evaluations. *Kaizen Teian 2* builds on that base to address in a practical way how to teach the principles of kaizen and proposal making, with further discussion on using proposal evaluation as a means of on-the-job training.

Kaizen is a Japanese word that has become part of the language in many Western companies; it means continuous incremental improvement of the standard way of work. This kind of creative improvement is something that every employee is capable of participating in — in fact, since a front-line employee is most familiar with the actual work, there is no better person to ask for improvement ideas.

The word *teian* means proposal or suggestion. Kaizen teian — a companywide system for implementing continuous improvement proposals from employees — is one of the most effective and widespread forms of kaizen activities in Japan. It is an organized way of bringing forth the ideas of each employee, no matter how small the improvement.

Kaizen Teian 2 offers concrete help for managers and supervisors charged with guiding the growth of such a suggestion system. The aim is to equip those managing kaizen efforts with the tools for teaching employees what kaizen and teian are all about. Each chapter in Parts 1 through 3 discusses a principle of doing kaizen or making a good proposal. Part 1 deals with basic concepts of kaizen — its focus on developing employee abilities, defining and solving workplace problems, dealing with causes rather than making repairs, and making sure that solutions deal with the *real* cause.

Part 2 delves into more specific main principles of kaizen. Chief among these is resourcefulness or ingenuity — achieving a result through clever use of resources at hand rather than large expenditures. Employees can learn how to be resourceful by dealing with issues that directly affect their work — like making their work less tiring, doing with one stroke what used to take several small motions, or mistake-proofing a process, to draw from examples in Chapter 6. As workers discover how kaizen can make their lives easier, they are naturally drawn to use their ideas in other ways.

Kaizen is also about finding simple, elegant solutions that attack the heart of a problem. One example from Chapter 7 involves the problem of cleaning up ticket-punch litter — thousands of tiny circles scattered all over the station floor. High-tech robots and electronic passcards were discussed as means to solve the litter problem, but the idea that won the day was an employee suggestion to install a small canister on the ticket punch to catch the circles — a simple and inexpensive solution.

Kaizen is also about ways to transfer skills quickly to newcomers. Chapter 8 describes how employees in a retail store gift-wrap department eliminated customer complaints about unskillful gift-wrap jobs by newer employees. Rather than requiring the new employees to go through a longer training course, the employees devised a system of standard box and wrapping paper sizes, with a template for positioning the box on the paper before wrapping. With this system, even new employees can wrap a box nicely on the first try. The standardized system turned out to be a much more effective teaching mechanism than extended training and was much less expensive.

Kaizen is about improvement of processes to reduce waste or unnecessary motion. Taken to its natural extension, the highest form of kaizen is find a way to eliminate a process altogether. This "ultimate kaizen" is discussed in Chapter 9.

Part 3 focuses on how to guide kaizen teian activities. As Chapter 10 points out, the point of kaizen is to develop the organization by developing the people within it. Kaizen is about building competent employees who can respond to circumstances, autonomously adjusting the course of their activities like "smart missiles."

This growth takes place through on-the-job training as supervisors and managers review proposals and coach employees in revising and implementing them. Chapter 11 presents a simple three-level system for reviewing proposals that makes a common framework for supervisors and employees to understand:

- what is required to make a high-quality proposal
- degrees of effectiveness in the way proposed countermeasures resolve problems
- new objectives to strive for.

Chapter 12 offers advice for supervisors and managers who wish to be effective leaders of a kaizen teian process. Most important is an attitude that genuinely cultivates the flowering of employee improvement ideas. Advice is given about what not to say, and *why*.

Part 4 of *Kaizen Teian 2* offers narrative case study examples from the experiences of employees in five different organizations — a bottling plant, an automotive component manufacturer, an agricultural coop, a circuit board plant, and an auto assembly plant. These examples show some of the principles introduced earlier in the book as they are applied to actual situations. These cases and the discussion questions at the end of each chapter are opportunities for discovering how you can adapt and apply the basic concepts to your own workplace.

We are pleased to bring you this second volume of our three-part series on managing the kaizen teian system. *Kaizen Teian 3: Sustaining Continuous Improvement Through Employee Suggestions* will conclude the series, presenting the natural evolution of the proposal system into a "kaizen reporting system" in which proposals are implemented first and written up later.

The material in these books was developed by Bunji Tozawa, managing editor with the Japan Human Relations Association (JHRA). Mr. Tozawa is a world-class expert on the kaizen teian system. He compiled the material that many of you know as *The Idea Book*, and has worked tirelessly to evolve the continuous improvement proposal system into the management process described in these books. In addition to writing and editing JHRA's monthly magazine, *Ingenuity and Inventions*, Mr. Tozawa also lectures and presents workshops in the United States and Europe as well as in Japan. We greatly appreciate his assistance, and that of Kenjiro Yamada, managing director of JHRA, in bringing about this translation.

Our thanks to Linda Topolsky, senior specialist, human resources for Nippondenso USA, for contributing an insightful foreword for this volume. Special recognition is due Mugi Hanao for assistance in clarifying the translation. Dorothy Lohmann managed the editorial preparation, with the assistance of Laura St. Clair (word processing), Christine Carvajal (manuscript editing), and Northwind Associates (indexing). Production was managed by Gayle Joyce, assisted by Michele Saar. The cover was designed by Joyce C. Weston.

Norman Bodek
Publisher

Karen R. Jones
TEI Series Editor

Foreword

A number of what I call "corporate self-help" books currently on the market reiterate a common business need: *companies must become more productive, faster, more responsive to the customer.* The global message of their authors rings loud and clear: to meet the increasingly competitive demands of the twenty-first-century marketplace, managers *must* solicit and use the input of employees at all levels of the organization. The impact of this message is visible in the dramatic new influx of participative management tools, like self-directed work teams, rapidly making their appearance in manufacturing and service sectors.

Continuous improvement suggestion systems are based on the management concepts of *kaizen*, meaning small, simple, incremental improvements, and *teian*, meaning development of employees through idea proposals. Kaizen teian — continuous improvement suggestion systems — stand in stark contrast to traditional suggestion systems that measure success relative to cost savings. The former have numerous advantages over their historical predecessors (see figure).

How Kaizen Systems Differ From Traditional Systems

Characteristics	Kaizen	Traditional
Purpose	• employee involvement and development • communication • economic benefits	• economic benefits
Focus	• many very small changes (e.g., revising a form • elimination of daily hassles	• few very large changes (e.g., changing a manufacturing process) • "breakthroughs"
Awards	• few dollars • merchandise	• usually thousands of dollars • cash
Participation	• 50% and higher • many ideas accepted	• 5% and lower • many ideas not accepted
Implementation	• employees implement most of own ideas • quick • suggestion = implemented improvement idea	• management, engineering driven • slow, drawn-out • employees less accountable • suggestion = improvement idea
Adoption rate	• near 100%	• approximately 25%
Administrator	• majority of time spent processing implemented ideas and issuing awards • specialist	• majority of time spent investigating unimplemented ideas and explaining "rejected" ones • manager
Suggestions received per year	• thousands	• hundreds
Highest award	• $2.00 - $10,000 (or merchandise valued at)	• $193,260
Motivators	• intrinsic satisfaction — personal development and recognition • frequent feedback and awards	• extrinsic rewards — money • infrequent

Simply put, traditional systems attempt to motivate by giving monetary awards on rare occasions to a few employees scattered throughout the work force. Such a system often does more harm than good because the majority of employee ideas are rejected, leading to mass negative attitudes toward management. The effectiveness of a kaizen system lies in the fact that it motivates by rewarding a much larger percentage of the work force on a much more frequent basis. This has a cumulative behavioral effect of improving attitudes, building trust, and boosting morale, which together become the foundation of an increasingly productive work force.

Increasing work force productivity is not the easiest thing to implement. Most books about it do a good job of telling managers *what* they should be doing, such as involving subordinates more. Their rhetoric, however, falls markedly short of describing *how* readers can actually carry out this command. *Kaizen Teian 2* picks up the dialogue by introducing readers to the fundamental elements of implementing and sustaining a continuous improvement suggestion system. Its format is very readable and its content indispensable to the cost-cutting, sociotechnical imperatives rapidly evolving in boardrooms around the world.

A number of concepts discussed in this timely book stand out as especially relevant for companies starting up new suggestion systems, and to those looking to improve systems that may already be in place:

- *Ideas are valuable only when they are implemented.* System administration can be simplified and participation maximized by defining a suggestion as an implemented improvement idea.
- *Increased productivity and profitability result from the accumulation of many small ideas.* Cultivation of large improvements without the small ones (perhaps otherwise construed as incidental) has little or no effect on changing the behaviors that ultimately impact productivity and profitability.

- *Suggester training is essential.* Most good systems train employees to teach basic policies and procedures. Stellar systems go beyond the basics to address such issues as how to question the status quo, how to solve problems more creatively, how to identify root causes in addition to symptomatic problems, and how to implement good ideas. In essence, successful suggestion systems seem to be moving toward incorporating the "what" with the "how."
- *Perceptions reign.* Effective systems change the way employees look at their jobs, and the methods used to accomplish even the simplest of tasks. They invoke a questioning demeanor: "Why do we do it this way?" "How could it be done better?" The best systems also affect employee perceptions of their own value to the company: "My ideas are important to management — I am a valuable asset."
- *Change is key.* There is always something to improve, through elimination, reduction, and overall revision of methods. *Kaizen Teian 2* offers valuable insight about teaching employees exactly *how* to eliminate, reduce, and revise.

Although the kaizen teian system is sometimes described by its Japanese name, its benefits are by no means limited to companies in Japan. Nippondenso Manufacturing U.S.A. in Battle Creek, Michigan, is among the many companies in the United States currently using a participative-style suggestion system.

In just two and a half years, Nippondenso's suggestion system has grown to be one of the most successful suggestion systems in the United States. Between January 1990 (its first year of operation) and June 1992, 75 percent of the 900 eligible suggesters submitted nearly 12,000 suggestions — all of which were *implemented* improvement ideas. In 1991 alone the system generated a net cost savings of $1.2 million.

The success of Nippondenso's program is insightful evidence that the American work force is overwhelmingly ready and willing to participate in the type of continuous improvement system outlined in *Kaizen Teian 2*. Many other companies share similar success stories of using kaizen systems to motivate and develop American workers.

Suggestion systems in the United States are transforming from backroom, side-office programs into full-fledged elements of business strategy. As a strategic tool, their role is rapidly becoming much more than an employee incentive plan; they now serve to develop employees' minds and abilities, to reward employees for their good ideas, and to significantly reduce operational costs for sponsor companies. Because it builds trust and makes everyone feel good about his or her unique contributions to the bottom line, a well-developed kaizen suggestion system can be one of the most powerful bridges ever built between labor and management in America. In this endeavor, *Kaizen Teian 2* is a valuable resource.

Linda Topolsky
Senior Specialist, Human Resources
Nippondenso Manufacturing U.S.A., Inc.

Preface

Four representative opinions of innovative proposals are often heard describing the present status of the kaizen teian movement:

1. There are no more seeds for new proposals.
2. We don't have any more ideas.
3. We are no longer in the kaizen stage.
4. We tried so hard to be innovative, and nothing was implemented.

Although opinions like these are often heard, continuous improvement will fail to make further advances if we just nod our heads in agreement. The purpose of this book is to do away with complaints that stress our supposed helplessness.

This book, however, is not simply a collection of suggestions from real life and advice that one might receive in a counseling office. It explains basic concepts and ways of thinking rather than trying to prescribe ways to accomplish certain ends or new perspectives for looking at things.

It is not designed as a method to treat symptoms of an illness or a collection of questions and answers. Instead, it asks questions like, "What do we mean by kaizen teian?" and "What methods can be used for making innovative proposals?" and presents the guiding principles of creative improvement proposals.

On the other hand, this is not to say that everything is in order once proposals are being made. Proposals are significant only if they are implemented and realized, so that they change the way we do our jobs. The purpose of this book is not merely to serve as a guide to proposal systems, but to present methods to change the way we do our jobs through proposals.

This book is compiled of a revised and reconstructed collection of special articles dealing with improvement proposal activity. The articles were published in a specialized magazine called *Ingenuity and Inventions*, a monthly magazine dedicated to the kaizen teian movement. Although it introduces examples of innovative proposals that were realized in many companies, the description of the proposals was shortened and dramatized. This is because the purpose of this book is not to introduce superficial examples of proposals, but to use practical examples to explain the principles and rules on which innovative proposals are based. A more concrete study of practical examples is offered in *Kaizen Teian 3* (forthcoming).

PART ONE

Basic Concepts of Kaizen

What is kaizen? Without clearly understanding what it is, we cannot practice kaizen or provide guidance for others. In this part of the book we consider the main concepts behind kaizen from the following four viewpoints.

1. Kaizen means developing abilities.
2. Kaizen means solving problems.
3. Kaizen means devising measures that deal with causes of problems.
4. Kaizen means devising measures that deal with the real causes of problems.

1

Kaizen Means Developing Abilities

In talking about kaizen, you often hear the words "methods for creative thinking," "idea generation," or "original thinking techniques." People sometimes talk about the need for "mental gymnastics" or "a change of creative pace." Exploring such subjects is not a waste of time when you're looking for creative ideas. It is probably better to think like this than to do nothing at all.

On the other hand, creativity enhancement techniques alone cannot replace a proper study of kaizen. They represent only a small part of continuous improvement, a part that in no way guarantees "good kaizen."

Creative thinking workshops usually have the following characteristics in common:

1. The group discusses assigned problems.
2. There is never a single solution to a problem; every problem is considered from various viewpoints, and various solutions are proposed.
3. Several methods are presented for getting beyond preconceptions and fixed ideas. Methods are introduced that help generate new ideas.

4. Unique or unorthodox solutions and decisions are praised.
5. A broad view of the situation is taken, so that group members become more adaptable to various interpretations of a complex situation.
6. Once agreement is reached on a solution, workers immediately begin implementation in their jobs.

Clearly, this process is pleasant and stimulating. It promotes a sense that many more new ideas will come to light this way. Unfortunately, it is not very useful in kaizen activity. What is written in books and discussed in seminars often bears little resemblance to reality. People who are initially enthusiastic about applying these methods to their improvement activities soon lose interest or question whether the methods really work on the job.

Why don't these methods ensure successful kaizen proposal activities? They are in the same league as "surefire methods for getting rich" or "how to make millions in real estate." The people who really know how to succeed draw on much more than little tips or tricks. They use a more fundamental approach, a method with substance to it. The same approach must be taken with kaizen activities.

THREE ESSENTIAL STRUCTURAL COMPONENTS OF KAIZEN

Real kaizen is made up of three essential components:

1. *Perceptiveness:* Discovering problems and pointing out what type of kaizen is required to fix them.
2. *Idea development:* Devising creative solutions to problems.
3. *Decision making, implementation, and effect:* Deciding which kaizen proposals are the best and which can be implemented, planning how to implement them, and then actually implementing them. The effect will follow.

Three Levels of Kaizen Teian Activities

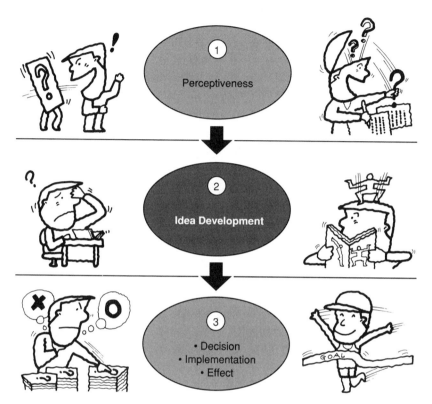

Creative thinking methods and exercises support only the second of these three essential elements.

Perceptiveness

The starting point of kaizen is a problem. If you don't have any problems, you don't need to do kaizen. If you have problems but don't notice them, you won't be motivated to make improvements. Only when a problem has been discovered can creative thinking, honed by past experience, start to play an important role.

Most of our education was designed to teach us how to solve problems that were assigned to us. Consequently, we grew up believing that problem solving means simply solving assigned problems. Such a concept is far too limited for the business environment. Here, the ability to *discover* problems is an essential precondition to problem solving.

Certainly, teaching new employees to solve assigned problems is very important in kaizen activity. At the initial stages, supervisors should make employees aware of areas where there are problems, give them hints about how to do kaizen, and assign tasks. At some point, however, new employees must learn to recognize tasks that need doing and to identify job-related problems on their own. This ability is the starting point of kaizen, because it is here that the worker begins to attack the problems inherent in the status quo.

Idea Development

Because this stage involves coming up with creative ideas and proposals, creative thinking methods and idea generation techniques are useful. They help you to free yourself from preconceived ideas and thereby enable you to study the problem from different angles.

Some people, however, seem to know everything about the theory of creative thinking yet hardly ever have practical ideas. On the other hand, you do not need to study such methods to come up with good ideas.

Making continuous improvement in your work is not like creating a breakthrough invention; it does not require the same amount of original thinking. The types of ideas we are talking about here generally are not things one would seek a patent for. For this reason, it is not necessary to cultivate and practice any specialized skills. Masaaki Imai notes in his book, *Kaizen*, that common sense is often all that is needed.

In kaizen, therefore, you don't have to understand complicated concepts like "change of creative pace" or "the power of originality"; anything you think about can become a proposal for improvement. An ordinary kaizen proposal is much better than a "creative" but impractical idea; it is probably going to be much easier to adopt and implement, which means that it is much more useful.

Decision, Implementation, and Effect

Another difference between kaizen and creative thinking methods is that only kaizen comprises a decision, implementation, and effect.

If mental exercise was the only thing needed, we could come up with a concept and be satisfied with that. But the real work of doing kaizen would be still ahead of us.

Kaizen is valuable only when it is implemented. Ideas that cannot be implemented or that fail to be realized are meaningless. That is why we must always ask ourselves how an idea can be implemented given present limitations. We must learn how to make a kaizen proposal into reality, and accept only ideas that meet this condition.

This aspect of kaizen activity distinguishes it from idea contests and competitions. Such contests, designed to attract and reward unique ideas, have little to do with kaizen activity. Realization and effect determine the ultimate value of kaizen.

Industrial activity is subject to many limitations, such as cost, quality, payment and delivery, safety, and so on. Ideas that ignore these limitations are useless. Kaizen involves ideas that clearly take into account these conditions. As managers, we need to understand the situation at our company and conditions at our workplace, and to make decisions that are based on this situation.

Whether or not they realize it, employees who take part in the kaizen proposal activities improve their judgment and implementation skills. Kaizen activity that does not include implementation and effect is no more than an interesting game. This game is not particularly useful for developing the employee skills that are important in industrial environment.

Three Essential Elements of Kaizen and Kaizen Teian Activity

	Basic idea	What is written up	Evaluation points	Objectives
Percep-tiveness	Noticing things	Problem areas, present situation	• "Creating" problems • Digging out problems • Becoming aware of problems • Dissatisfaction with present conditions	Participation
Idea Develop-ment	A resourceful solution	An improvement proposal	• Looking for causes • Study and investigation • Creative thinking • Solution based on a new perspective	Skill development
• Decision • Implemen-tation • Effect	Realization	Results	• Effort in implementing • Follow-up • Significance of effect	Effect

Perceptiveness and Implementation Outweigh Creative Thinking

Creative thinking is not the only important component of kaizen activity. Indeed, the role of creative thinking methods has been greatly overemphasized.

In determining how to provide guidance and education for kaizen activity, you must first clearly formulate what is required for kaizen activity, how to develop skills through education and guidance, and what the objectives are. You should recognize that the abilities first to identify problems and then to select and implement solutions are critical to the development of job-related skills and to promotion of kaizen in the workplace. As you develop review standards and educational activities, it is probably a good idea to pay more attention to these aspects of kaizen than to creative thinking methods.

THREE STEPS NECESSARY FOR PROMOTING PROPOSALS AND DEVELOPING ABILITIES

The ultimate objective of kaizen activity is to develop in all employees the three skills previously discussed:

1. Perceptiveness
2. Idea development
3. Decision making and implementation

A kaizen teian (improvement proposal) system does not need to be perfect from its outset. In fact, it would be unreasonable to demand perfection from a kaizen system that has just been introduced. Being too strict with people who are writing improvement proposals for the first time usually provokes a negative reaction.

Although ultimately you will ask employees for well-prepared proposals that include the three main elements, a proposal system must be promoted step-by-step. It might also be useful to deal with each process separately, from perception of problems to implementation.

Step 1: Developing Perceptiveness

This first step requires employees to take a good look at the workplace to see if something in the work needs improvement. Perhaps there are quality problems, or maybe awkward procedures make the work difficult. At this stage, the focus is on discovering or identifying problems, so these are the activities that will be evaluated.

During the same stage you will be encouraging all employees to participate in improvement activity. At the very least, you want employees to identify problems and irregularities, write down the things they are not happy about, and bring hidden problems out in the open. This activity alone is of great importance because it brings out valuable information.

Step 2: Developing Good Solutions

At this stage employees are trying to devise solutions to the problems they discovered during the first stage. This is when independent thinking and new ideas can be very useful. It is important to view each problem from different angles, to see various aspects of problems. One person can do this alone. However, three people will have the advantage of knowing more about the problem, and groups are useful for exchanges of opinions. Also effective are various techniques that promote creative thinking, such as brainstorming and affinity diagrams, and the seven QC tools.

Proposals presented during this stage are sometimes called idea proposals, or unimplemented proposals. At this stage, no "effect" value should be assigned. It is possible, however, to evaluate the best ideas that have been proposed. Remember that a significant part of the kaizen proposal process is research, analysis, and thinking.

Step 3: Developing Decision-making and Implementation Skills

In old-style suggestion systems, a person would write a proposal on a piece of paper and put it in a suggestion box. Such a system allows employees to express creative thinking but not much more. It was left to higher-ups (upper managers and review committee members) to review suggestions and decide which ones to adopt. This was an uncomfortable situation for employees. The percentage of proposals implemented under such a system was low, so it was not very effective.

Three Stages of Kaizen

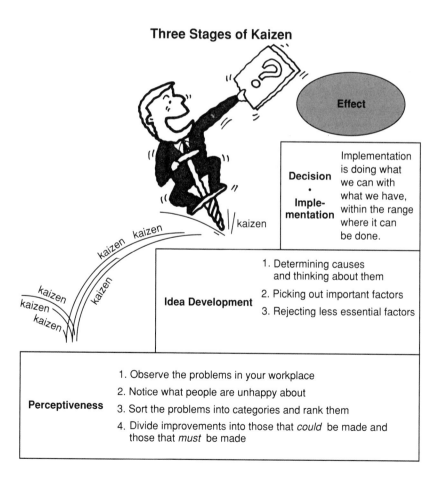

Effect

Decision
•
Imple-mentation

Implementation is doing what we can with what we have, within the range where it can be done.

Idea Development

1. Determining causes and thinking about them
2. Picking out important factors
3. Rejecting less essential factors

Perceptiveness

1. Observe the problems in your workplace
2. Notice what people are unhappy about
3. Sort the problems into categories and rank them
4. Divide improvements into those that *could* be made and those that *must* be made

Thus it became necessary to give the innovators themselves the responsibility for reviewing their proposals and making decisions. Whereas the old system placed little reliance on employees, the new system based on implemented improvements required employees to make decisions and implement proposals.

DISCUSSION QUESTIONS

How does kaizen differ from creativity enhancement methods?

What are the three main components of kaizen activity?

2

Kaizen Means Solving Problems

The seeds of continuous improvement exist anyplace a problem exists. A problem is the launching pad for kaizen.

But what happens when people say that they have run out of problems to work on, or that there is no longer a need to improve anything? Having done kaizen for a while, they believe that they have done everything there is to do. When such opinions are expressed, even supervisors and kaizen activity promoters start doubting its usefulness. Once there are no problems, they reason, there is no need for kaizen. But have they really run out of problems?

PROBLEMS: A TEXTBOOK DEFINITION

What do we mean when we say the word *problem*? It is a word we are so used to that we don't think about its real meaning.

The question can be answered in many ways. Some might see a problem as "something that bothers us," or "something that has to be solved," or "something that causes inconvenience."

More exacting people might say that a problem is "a discrepancy between the present situation and our objectives" or "a discrepancy between our objectives and the actual results." These are textbook definitions.

But textbook knowledge does not go far enough in explaining what problems mean in terms of improving our own work or workplace. In such terms, we might categorize problems according to three types:

1. Those that are noticed or discovered
2. Those that are dug out
3. Those that are "created"

Problems that Are Noticed or Discovered

This type of problem is the easiest one to define. It can be described as a situation that should not exist, or a discrepancy between an undesirable situation and a desirable situation (or the standard).

There are always people who pay little attention to problems, as well as people who never notice them at all. These people either have no standards by which to recognize a desirable state or do not understand the actual situation.

Unless you have a standard that specifies the quality of product required, the cost of manufacturing, and other characteristics, you will not be bothered by any problems, no matter what you do or how you do it. That is, if you do not understand the desirable state, you won't discern any problems. Even if you have a standard, you will still miss problems if you don't pay attention to the current level of product quality or business results. If you ignore reality, you become blind and deaf to problems.

Conversely, with awareness of the desired state and attention to the current state, you can recognize discrepancies, or problems. Therefore, problem awareness has three components:

- being aware of the desired state (having a standard)
- understanding the present situation
- being aware of the discrepancy between the desired state and the present situation

When the discrepancy between the present situation and the desired state is obvious to you, we say that you "notice" the problem. When the discrepancy is not obvious except to the very observant, we say that you "discover" or "identify" the problem.

Problems that Are Dug Out

Imagine that your job and workplace have reached the desired state, or standard. This may be your situation today, but what about tomorrow, next month, or next year? There is no guarantee that this situation will continue forever. No matter how things are going today, they can all too easily slip back into the undesirable zone. Indeed, continuing on the same track may in itself create a problem in the future. In such a situation, problems must be "dug out."

Unlike noticing and discovering problems that already exist, digging out problems requires the ability to imagine, predict, and accurately assess a situation. You must be able to discern future trends in present circumstances. This kind of kaizen is also called *preventive kaizen*.

Problems that Are Created

The first two types of problems both involve a discrepancy between the present situation and the desired situation. Moreover, they both feed into the common perception of problems as things that, once found, should be solved. This perception flows naturally from the passive attitude that a problem is something presented to us by others. That notion in turn goes hand in hand with the idea that standards are things determined by managers and other higher-ups in the company.

Differing from the first two types of problems in both respects is the third type of problem — the problem we "create" by applying our own standards. We create a problem — in a positive sense — when we define targets on a level that is higher than our present level. To preserve the distinction between this and passive problems that either exist already or will exist in the future, we can think of created problems as active improvement "tasks."

Three Types of Problems

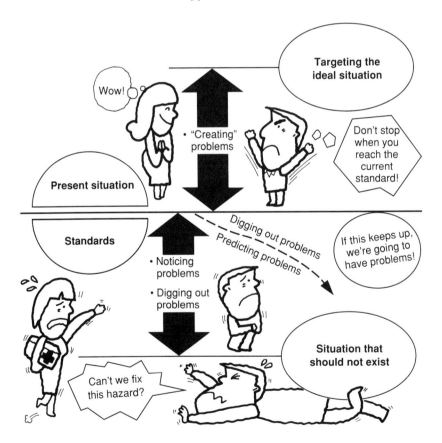

As long as we define targets and standards on the present level, we have no problems. We can do this when we are content with things as they are. But we live in a world where everything is in constant flux and where the competition is continually changing the rules to outperform us. We have no choice but to change our own standards. Even if we are happy with the present situation, external factors will prevent us from being happy with it forever.

Although we may have no problems with product quality, cost, and so on, when the competition raises its standards to meet customer demands, ultimately we will also have to raise our standards as well. Like it or not, we will have to deal with the problems that will crop up.

The question is whether to take a passive approach, dealing with problems as they arise, or to take the initiative ourselves by formulating new standards and targets for a new era. The difference between those two approaches is the difference between people who are hounded by problems and those who chase after problems.

Having No Problems Is a Problem

People who say that they have run out of seeds of improvement or that they have no problems belong to one of three categories:

- Those who do not notice problems
- Those who cannot foresee and predict problems
- Those who are content with things as they are

In each case, however, the real problem is the belief that there are no problems. Those who understand the kaizen proposal system know that it is impossible to have no problems.

As employees become more experienced with problem solving, their managers often complain, "If only they were able to notice the problems," or "I wish they could visualize the potential problems," or "We need people who can set improvement tasks for themselves."

After solving all problems perceived through the passive approach, people may feel that nothing more needs to be done. But that is true only when the existing standard applies. As soon as a higher level of standards and targets is set, problems (tasks to be achieved) will crop up. People who say there are no problems are revealing only that their target is low and that they are not serious in their determination to improve things. Setting a higher target sows the seeds of many improvements.

It's nonsense to say that we have no problems. Our first problem is that we think that way — we're content with the status quo! We must set more challenging targets.

WHY PEOPLE SAY THERE ARE NO PROBLEMS

There is no point in browbeating people who are not interested in kaizen or who "have no problems." What is required is to analyze the underlying causes. "*Why* is this person content with the way things are? *Why* is she unwilling to change the way she does her work?" Such questions may lead us to the truth that, in fact, this person is *not* happy with the status quo. She may indeed see problems but be reluctant to rock the boat. So she conceals her real feelings.

We can motivate this person to come up with kaizen proposals only by eliminating the underlying causes of this conduct. To do so, we use two approaches.

1. We explain what a problem is, theoretically and logically.
2. We search for the real feelings behind such a person's superficial attitude.

We must also consider structural factors behind the situation, such as the work environment, attitudes within the company, and supervisors' reactions.

DISCUSSION QUESTIONS

What is the textbook definition of a problem?

What three types of problems exist in kaizen activity?

What is meant by problems that are "created"?

Why is it impossible to have no problems in a kaizen proposal system?

3

Kaizen Means Dealing with Causes

THE DIFFERENCE BETWEEN KAIZEN AND REPAIR

Not long ago, it was common to see steel plates used to cover gutters on the factory floor. Most of the time these steel plates were warped and did not lie flat.

The employees' response to this interesting phenomenon varied widely. Some people walked over the plates every day without noticing anything. Others did notice but did not concern themselves with the problem. One day it occurred to someone that, "someone is going to trip on a crooked plate and get hurt," whereupon the person notified the company offices. When the company took no action, this person picked up a hammer and straightened the plates.

The Vicious Cycle of "Fixing Things Up"

A company likes to have workers who will solve problems on their own. Clearly, they make better employees than those who never notice or do anything. We admire people like that — but that activity is not kaizen. Rather, it is simple repair.

It is not a bad thing to straighten up a warped plate. The next day, however, it will likely be warped again, and someone will have to fix it one more time. And the day after that the cycle will be repeated. Such a cycle never ends.

Why was the steel plate repaired rather than improved? The reason is that the person forgot to ask "*Why* is this steel plate warped?" Instead, the employee dealt only with the symptoms: "Since it is warped, I will straighten it." Nothing was done about the causes of the situation.

Since the causes were not eliminated, the problem is bound to continue. No matter how many times the plate is straightened out, the warping will recur. On the other hand, if the worker asked *why* the plate was warped, that would have been a wonderful example of kaizen.

REAL KAIZEN WON'T BREAK THE NEXT DAY

This "cause" that we keep talking about is not such a difficult concept. No elaborate theory is required to find out what causes a problem. Anyone can do it.

The cause of the warping in our example was that trucks were passing over that were too heavy for the plates. Knowing the cause, we can find ways to cope with the problem. We could (1) prohibit heavy trucks from passing over the plate, or (2) use stronger plates. Both of these solutions are good improvements because they eliminate the cause. Either solution will keep the plates from warping again. If proposal 1 is feasible, it would be the better idea; it is the simplest and most efficient form of innovation. On the other hand, if it is important to maintain access to the road, it will be necessary to use the other approach — increasing the strength of the steel plates.

Several methods could be used to strengthen the plates. A thicker steel plate or concrete covers could do the job. Either solution would cost some money, but if the budget allowed, it could be done. Since the measure deals with the cause of the problem, the cause is eliminated, and that is the end of the warped plates.

In reality, however, things are not so simple. Most companies do not have unlimited budgets for changes like this; other things tend to have priority when it comes to funding. Unless there is an emergency, expenditures are often postponed.

So it was at the factory in question. Requests to replace the plates with thicker ones or with concrete covers were "taken under consideration" and shelved. In the meantime, the warped plate was repaired again and again.

One day, another employee lost patience in waiting for an answer and money to do something about the plates. His breakthrough was to brace the edges and corners of the gutter covers with steel feet. With these in place, even heavy trucks could pass over the gutter without bending the plates. The problem was finally solved.

Using measures that deal with causes does not mean that there is only one solution or one means that can be used. When there is enough money, just about any problem can be solved easily. But if money isn't available, low-cost approaches must be used. That involves more brain work.

PREVENTION IS BETTER THAN THE CLEVEREST REPAIR

Kaizen means devising measures that deal with causes of problems. Measures that fail to take into account the causes and deal only with the symptoms are called repairs.

Of course, a temporary fix may still be better than doing nothing at all. It is better to use an inadequate solution than to pretend a problem is not there. Problems that remain ignored often cause accidents or damage, and therefore become bigger problems.

After taking temporary measures, however, we have to find the causes and devise more permanent countermeasures. Real causes can be dealt with only by kaizen. Unless the causes

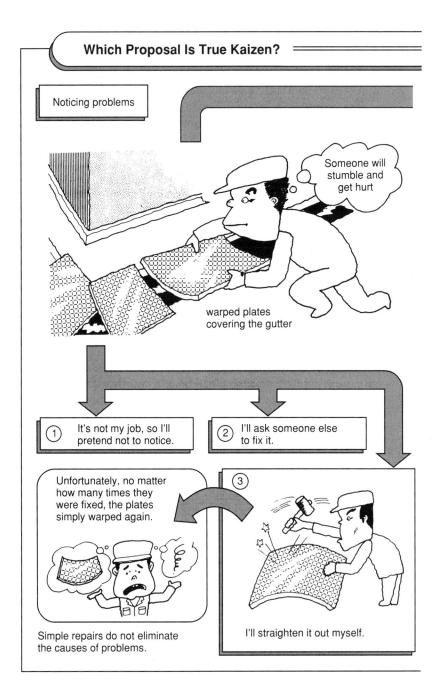

Kaizen Means Measures That Deal with Causes

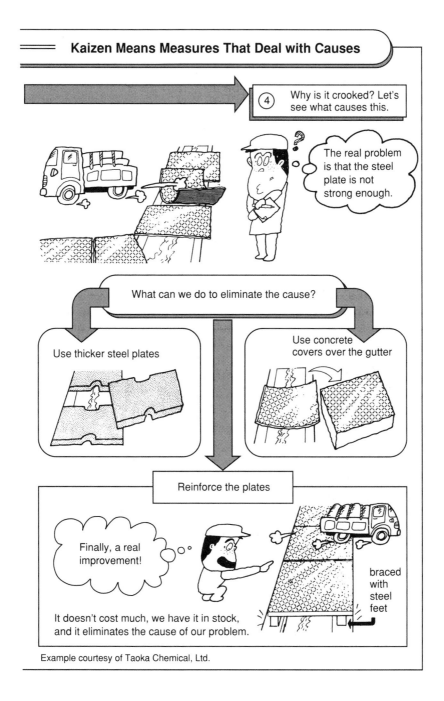

④ Why is it crooked? Let's see what causes this.

The real problem is that the steel plate is not strong enough.

What can we do to eliminate the cause?

Use thicker steel plates

Use concrete covers over the gutter

Reinforce the plates

Finally, a real improvement!

It doesn't cost much, we have it in stock, and it eliminates the cause of our problem.

braced with steel feet

Example courtesy of Taoka Chemical, Ltd.

are eliminated, the same problem and inconvenience will keep arising.

Why Do the Pants Keep Ripping?

Imagine a child who keeps ripping his pants. There are several ways to deal with this problem.

Some parents might say, "It's all right; just throw them away" or "I'll buy a new pair of pants for you anyway, so just get rid of these." Families with unlimited financial means can afford to treat the incident as a trivial thing. When that is the case, there is no problem and thus no need for improvement.

But let's say that the family is not wealthy enough to simply replace the ripped pants with new ones. Perhaps the child's grandmother offers to mend the rip. This solves the temporary problem of ripped pants but does not solve the problem of *why* the pants got ripped.

There is a reason for everything. In this case, maybe the pants got snagged on a nail, or maybe they were too small for the child. Unless the measures taken address the cause, even the best darning in the world will be useless. If the pants are too small, even tight darning won't prevent them from coming apart again in the seams.

Unfortunately, the grandmother doesn't consider the causes. When the pants rip again, she thinks only of better ways to repair them — maybe a thicker patch, or perhaps double stitching. Or maybe she should use a sewing machine. But using countermeasures that don't address the cause of the problem is like shooting in the dark. Occasionally you may hit the target, but the method is extremely inefficient.

Every day in our jobs, we think in the same narrow terms that the grandmother in our example used. If we handle a complaint skillfully, we think we've done enough. Once an error is corrected, we often think that we don't have to worry anymore. Thus the same problem will arise again and again. The same

Repair versus Kaizen

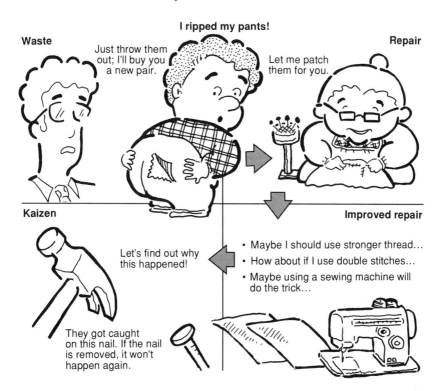

wastes, irregularities, and irrationalities will appear endlessly. Another factory section may be making the same mistake, and new complaints will arise.

Repair means restoring abnormal situations such as breakdowns, complaints, and accidents to normal ones. This is better than leaving problems as they are, but it is no more than returning to square one. We have forgotten to ask, "Why did this mistake happen?" and "What caused this problem?"

Kaizen, on the other hand, means devising countermeasures that deal with the cause of the problem. Such countermeasures are designed to prevent the problem from occurring again.

SAFETY IMPROVEMENT BEGINS WITH A SEARCH FOR CAUSES

The rule that kaizen means creating measures that deal with the causes of problems can also be applied to the improvement of safety problems. Needless to say, the best countermeasures for accidents and disasters are prediction and prevention. No matter how attentive we are, however, it is impossible to prevent all accidents. We are only human, and minor troubles are inevitable.

On the other hand, whether a small accident is contained and minimized or turns into a bigger problem depends on whether we pursue its causes or ignore them.

Six Ways of Responding to Accidents

Depending on the way they respond to a minor workplace accident, people can be sorted into six types.

The See-no-evil Type

The see-no-evil worker says of such an accident: "It is nothing serious; it's not even really an accident. Countermeasures? I've got so much to do. I don't really have time."

The Jaded Type

The jaded worker responds, "Oh no, not another accident! I am sick of this. Well, it was to be expected, given how busy we are. No wonder we have accidents, with the kind of equipment we're using. When no one cares about safety rules, this is bound to happen."

The Comforting Type

The comforting type of worker might say, "Boy, I'm glad it wasn't a big accident. From now on we have to be really careful.

No one intended to harm anyone, so let's just be glad that nothing serious happened, and pay more attention from now on."

The I-told-you-so Type

The I-told-you-so type responds in an accusing fashion: "Didn't I tell you? Who is responsible for this? No wonder; when we don't follow the rules to the letter, something like this is bound to happen!" These people become red in the face and make a lot of noise about an accident, but they don't undertake any concrete countermeasures. After the excitement goes down, they pretend that nothing happened.

The Cause-tracing Type

The cause-tracing type asks: "Why did the accident happen? What conditions made it possible?" He or she then attempts to determine the relationship between the causes of an accident and real conditions.

The Preventing Type

The preventing type tries to figure out what measures should be taken to make sure the accident will not happen again.

If Causes Are Not Eliminated, the Same Thing Will Happen Again

Next, let's predict how the six types of responders might react after a second accident.

The See-no-evil Type

The see-no-evil worker not only will not help prevent accidents but increases the probability that they will happen. Even if the accident involved a death, this person would shrug it off

Does Your Proposal Address the Cause of the Problem?

Level	Description
Demands	• It's crooked ⟶ let's ask someone to fix it. • It's dirty ⟶ let's have it cleaned. • We have a problem ⟶ someone should do something. Unless I can solve a problem on my own, I will never understand what really caused the problem.
Repairs	• It's crooked ⟶ let's straighten it out. • It's dirty ⟶ let's clean it. • It is bothering us ⟶ let's fix it. Even if I can wrestle with a problem on my own, if I don't know the cause, my solution will be only temporary.
Kaizen	• It's crooked ⟶ let's attack the reason for it. • It's dirty ⟶ let's eliminate what makes it dirty. • It's bothering us ⟶ let's get rid of the cause of the problem. We determine the cause, then carry out the counter-measures that can be implemented.

and say something like, "Compared to war, this is nothing." Such an attitude makes the prospect for better safety hopeless.

The Jaded Type

The jaded worker expresses frustration at "another accident" but continues to do nothing about the situation. The accidents will never stop this way.

The Comforting Type

The comforting worker continues to remind others that "we were lucky this time but there is no guarantee that we will be lucky next time." This type of person contributes to dangerous situations instead of eliminating them while they are small. He or she will take action only after a disaster happens, when it is too late.

The I-told-you-so Type

This type of worker continues to make noise about accidents but never takes action against them. Whatever caused the problem is still there, waiting to cause another accident. The danger here is that we get used to the noise and unconsciously follow a path to a serious accident.

The Cause-tracing and Preventing Types

The effect of the first four responses is the same — the accident will happen again. Whether the words are "Let's be careful," "Let's pay attention," or "Let's be thorough," they are nothing but talk. As long as nothing is done to eliminate the dangerous factors, accidents will recur.

Only types 5 and 6 would try to eliminate the dangerous factors to prevent a recurrence. They actually create countermeasures to ensure that an accident will not happen. They are doing kaizen.

If an accident happened where you work, what would be your attitude? Would it be similar to types 1 through 4, or would it be more like types 5 and 6? Your position may considerably influence safety in your company.

Danger can be prevented easily while still in its initial stage. Hazardous situations should be eliminated while injuries

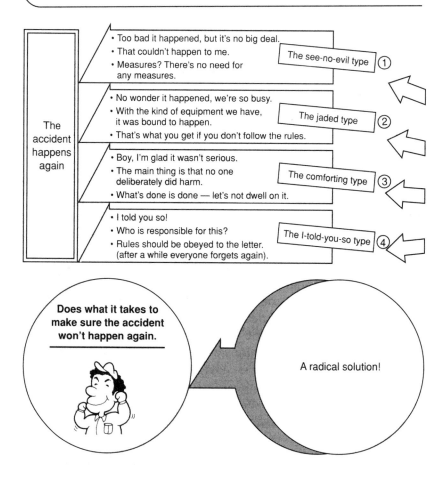

When an Accident Happens

The accident happens again

- Too bad it happened, but it's no big deal.
- That couldn't happen to me.
- Measures? There's no need for any measures.

The see-no-evil type ①

- No wonder it happened, we're so busy.
- With the kind of equipment we have, it was bound to happen.
- That's what you get if you don't follow the rules.

The jaded type ②

- Boy, I'm glad it wasn't serious.
- The main thing is that no one deliberately did harm.
- What's done is done — let's not dwell on it.

The comforting type ③

- I told you so!
- Who is responsible for this?
- Rules should be obeyed to the letter. (after a while everyone forgets again).

The I-told-you-so type ④

Does what it takes to make sure the accident won't happen again.

A radical solution!

and damage are still minor. Genuine kaizen involves creating countermeasures that ensure that dangerous circumstances are detected early and nipped in the bud.

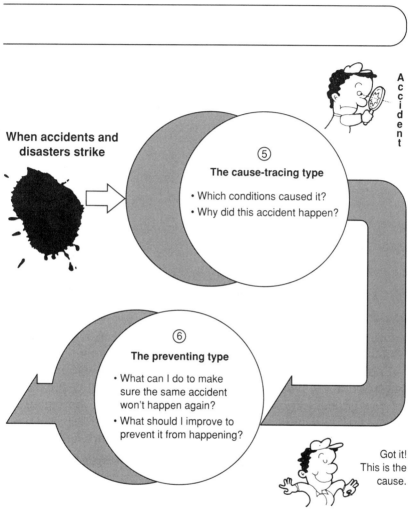

When accidents and disasters strike

⑤ The cause-tracing type
- Which conditions caused it?
- Why did this accident happen?

Accident

⑥ The preventing type
- What can I do to make sure the same accident won't happen again?
- What should I improve to prevent it from happening?

Got it! This is the cause.

DISCUSSION QUESTIONS

What is the difference between kaizen and repair?

What is the best way to respond to a problem in the workplace?

4

Kaizen Is a Solution that Deals with the Real Cause

If you look closely at the labels on bottled beer from the Asahi Brewing Company, you can see two short lines in the top right corner. These marks are the product of kaizen activity to improve the labeling process.

A labeler is a high-performance machine that revolves at a high speed. It is capable of sticking labels onto several hundred bottles a minute. Although the device that feeds the labels holds a considerable number of them, the supply runs out frequently. The operator then has to load another batch of labels.

At that point, mistakes sometimes occurred. Without realizing it, the operator sometimes loaded labels into the machine wrong side up. Once switched on, the machine would stick blank labels onto the bottles at great speed. The operator would rush to turn off the machine, but by then it was too late. The only thing to do was to take all the bottles off the line and remove the labels.

Unfortunately, this incident tended to happen most often in the summer, the peak production season. When it did, the supervisor went crazy. "Who did this? Don't you know we've got to run the machine constantly to keep up with our quota?" The operator who made the mistake would be so embarrassed that he was ready to disappear.

The operators in charge of supplying labels worked nervously during the summer months. A sign was posted reminding everyone to load the labels correctly.

This rather feeble method of control might still be in place if there had been no kaizen activities at the brewery. As it was, however, quality control and kaizen activities were strong at Asahi; thus it was not surprising that employees submitted various kaizen proposals to resolve the problem.

A Common Error in Loading Labels

GOOD IDEAS THAT ARE HARD TO IMPLEMENT

All of the proposed countermeasures dealt with the cause of the problem. One was a well-reasoned preventive measure: "If the labels and the label holder are asymmetrical, the machine will not accept them when they are set into the machine wrong side up. The operator will become aware of the mistake right away."

Another idea was clear and easy to understand: "Mistakes occur because the labels have a printed side and a blank side. If both sides of the labels were printed, no mistakes could occur, and we would have no problems."

Still another proposal used high-technology, suggesting the application of a sensor that would detect the wrong side of the labels, sound an alarm, and stop the machine.

All of these proposals were excellent ideas. If they could have been implemented easily, the problem would have been solved. Life is rarely that easy, however.

It would not be simple to change the design of the label, as the first proposal would require. Similarly, printing on both sides could not be implemented without incurring high costs for the printing and special adhesives. The sensor would also cost money. Budgetary constraints prevented the implementation of these ideas.

In most companies this would have been the end of the matter. The employees would grumble, "We've submitted several good ideas, but the company hasn't done anything to implement them." The brewery, however, has a strong tradition of kaizen. The employees knew from years of experience that when you hit a dead end, you go back to the beginning and start again. The improvement group who worked with the labeler tried one more time to find the "real reason" behind mistakes in loading labels.

WHAT IS THE REAL CAUSE?

The first response people usually give when asked why they made a mistake is something like "I was in a hurry," "I got flustered," or "I was busy with something else." If we stick with this level of explanation for the cause, our solutions will go no higher than that. The response might be signs advising workers to "Slow down!" or requests for additional staff, neither of which solves the problem.

It is more fruitful to take the question one step further. Let's ask *why* we make mistakes when we are in a hurry or flustered, *why* we get confused when we are busy. The real reason we make mistakes is not because we are flustered, in a hurry, or too busy, but because we are doing the job wrong in the first place. Once we know the real cause of the problem, we can set our minds to changing the way of doing the job so that mistakes do not occur, even when we are busy, in a hurry, or flustered.

SIMPLE SOLUTIONS ARE THE BEST KAIZEN

The workers at the brewery asked themselves the next question about the misloaded labels: "Why do we make mistakes when we are in a hurry?" They discovered that they made the mistake because they had no way of knowing which way the labels were facing without leaning over to check. That was the key.

Without craning their necks to look, the workers couldn't check the way they were inserting the labels. Once this was understood, it became plain that the real countermeasure was to change the way of doing the job so that the workers could check the direction of the labels without having to lean over.

By delving to this level of the problem, the workers were able to see the solution clearly. In this case, they suggested that marks be printed on the labels so that they would make a con-

What Is the Real Reason?

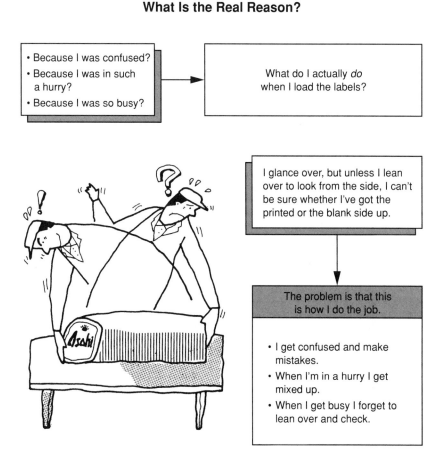

- Because I was confused?
- Because I was in such a hurry?
- Because I was so busy?

What do I actually *do* when I load the labels?

I glance over, but unless I lean over to look from the side, I can't be sure whether I've got the printed or the blank side up.

The problem is that this is how I do the job.

- I get confused and make mistakes.
- When I'm in a hurry I get mixed up.
- When I get busy I forget to lean over and check.

tinuous line when the labels were stacked together. That way, if the line on the labels is in front of the operator, then the labels are facing the right direction. Even when workers are in a hurry, it is easier to avoid mistakes. They no longer have to strain themselves to check the labels, so the checking gets done. Thanks to a couple of lines, the problem was eliminated, and mistakes no longer occur.

A Simple Mistake-proofing Idea

When the labels are correctly positioned, the marks create an easy-to-check stripe along the side of the stack of labels.

A couple of marks printed on the corner keep me from making a mistake.

A WEAK EFFORT PRODUCES WEAK KAIZEN

Compare the idea of adding a mark to the label with the earlier proposals to change the shape of the label, print on both sides, or install a sensor. Clearly, the mark idea is the more realistic and implementable solution. The critical difference, however, is in the degree to which the problem was pursued. If analysis of the problem is taken only to a halfway point, the countermeasure will likewise be only a halfway solution.

If the countermeasure is too elaborate for the problem, it will be difficult to implement, and even if implemented, the benefit may not be worth the effort. The closer we get to the heart of the problem, however, the easier it becomes to address it with a suitable set of countermeasures. These improvements are usually easy to implement and (more important) bring immediate results.

Those who had argued for more expensive ideas were no doubt embarrassed by the simplicity of the final solution.

GOOD KAIZEN COMES FROM PEOPLE CLOSE TO THE WORK

Anyone could have thought of installing a sensor, because that method is applied in many situations. The idea of marking the labels, however, could have been conceived only by someone who actually worked in the bottle-labeling workplace. In the kaizen teian system, proposals are based on firsthand knowledge of the job. Unless we understand every detail of how we do our job, we will not be able to come up with proper countermeasures.

This is the defining point of kaizen proposal activity. We do not need general kaizen, which can be practiced by anyone, but ideas that can come only from the people close to the work. That type of kaizen is truly valuable.

When the brewery employees recognized that the mistake could be eliminated if a line were made along the stack of labels, they made a proposal to add small marks next to the company emblem when new labels were printed. This idea was implemented right away.

With any proposal, the expenditures and risks have to be weighed against the benefits. If a proposal requires that significant changes be made, the company will naturally be cautious. Suggestions that call for more workers or new machinery are apt to be shelved, under the promise that the company will "think about it." In the final analysis, good results obtained from an easy-to-implement idea argue most persuasively.

DISCUSSION QUESTIONS

What does it mean to find the "real cause" of a problem?

Why are simple solutions preferable to elaborate ones?

PART TWO

Principles of Kaizen

How can we achieve better kaizen? The case studies presented in this part of the book show the importance of five principles of kaizen:

- Kaizen requires resourcefulness.
- Kaizen requires teaching people to be resourceful.
- Kaizen means pursuing the purpose.
- Kaizen requires a transfer of know-how.
- Kaizen sometimes means eliminating something.

5

Kaizen Requires Resourcefulness

Although the Japanese characters for *resourcefulness* and *hard work* are similar, these two approaches to improvement lead to very different results.

"Where there's a will, there's a way," the saying goes. This is a catchy phrase, but it does not tell the whole story. It leaves out a step between the "will" and the "way." Those of us who are not superheroes need something more than simple will to get the job done. That "something" is usually hard work. For us, the saying could be rephrased as "will plus hard work equals results."

According to this equation, to increase the results, we have to work harder. Willpower, stamina, and patience are in themselves not enough. However, merely working harder will not achieve unlimited results for us, either.

That is because hard work is not the only component standing between will and results. The other component to keep in mind is *resourcefulness*. Hard work means unflagging effort but not necessarily changing our approach to the work. Resourcefulness, on the other hand, means taking a close look at the methods we use. It means asking ourselves the questions

"What would be the best way to do this?" "What other approaches could we try?" "Is there a method better than the one we're using?" In other words, it means using kaizen. Kaizen entails figuring out what conditions lie between the will and the results, making a strategy based on what is needed, and then implementing that strategy.

This method does not always work immediately. Ultimately, however, you will see very different results depending on whether you continue to simply work hard or to use resourcefulness.

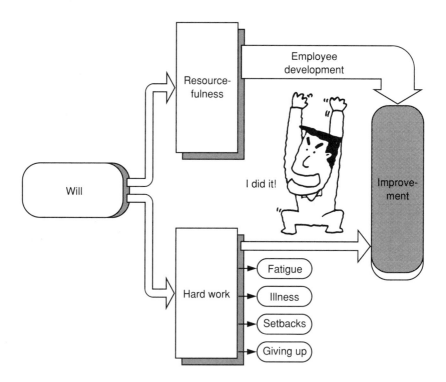

NOTHING CHANGES WITHOUT RESOURCEFULNESS

Let's assume that a job involves work that is exacting and difficult to do. Employees new to the workplace are likely to voice their complaints and dissatisfaction about it. The ways in which their fellow workers and supervisors react to these complaints can be sorted into two broad categories.

One group of people stresses hard work. These people tell the unhappy new workers, "We had to do this when we were in your position. What are you whining about? You get paid to put up with this." Through patience and perseverance, the new employees would also get used to the difficult job. But because they do the job the same way their predecessors did, productivity would not increase. In due course, other new employees would be hired. The cycle would start again, and the same level of productivity would be maintained for another year.

The "hard work" group includes more than just these hard-liners. There is also the "soft-liner" who expresses understanding, saying, "Oh, I know it's really difficult." This type points to the "fatigue" factor. But people in this group only talk about fatigue, so nothing changes. Neither the soft-liner nor the hard-liner facilitates the development of human potential and progress in the workplace.

People who emphasize resourcefulness take an active approach to problems in the workplace. Their response is likely to be, "What can we do about it?" and "Let's try to do kaizen." If the supervisors are good managers, they will encourage this approach: "Why don't we try this method?" or "It might be possible to use this method." In a stricter work environment, the employee might hear, "It's up to you to think about it and find a solution; be resourceful." The resourceful group also has a hard-line and a soft-line faction, but in both factions the emphasis is on resourcefulness and kaizen.

How does such a work environment influence the employees? They will learn from experience that resourcefulness can make their work more pleasant, faster, more accurate, and safer. With each successful result, the level of kaizen will rise. Moreover, many people will benefit from the successful experience. Those who see the good results will be inspired to practice kaizen and be resourceful. Eventually, the way things are done will change; indeed, the whole workplace will change.

The progress made through resourcefulness will be far greater than that made through patience and endurance. In the old days, when there were few changes anyway, patience and endurance might have been justified. Under the old apprentice system, the greatest virtues were having patience and doing whatever the boss or senior apprentice told you to do. Doing things differently or in a more innovative way would be criticized as laziness or impudence. In this era of change and diversification, however, resourcefulness is more important to progress than hard work.

A LITTLE INGENUITY GOES A LONG WAY TOWARD SOLVING PROBLEMS

A common complaint in companies is that people do not stick to the rules that have been agreed on. For instance, you hear that "they don't maintain prescribed operating procedure; they just do whatever they feel like doing," or that "people don't return tools to the place where they borrowed them, even though that's the rule. That's sloppy."

Human society can be broken down into two kinds of people: those who create the rules and those who follow (or don't follow) these rules. There would be no problem if people could set their own standards and then abide by them, like an autonomous work group.

In most situations, however, these responsibilities are handled separately. All too often, the party that makes the rules

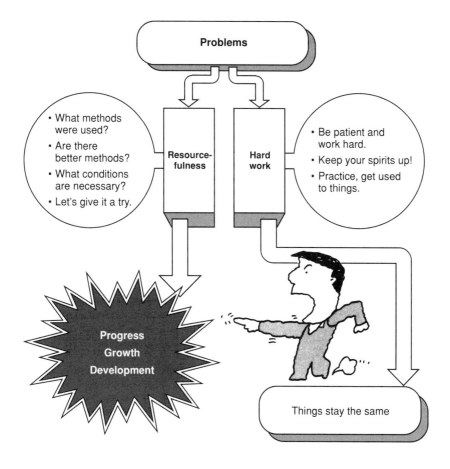

does so without giving much thought to the conditions of the environment (here, the workplace) in which those rules are to be followed. As a result, the rule soon loses any relevancy it may once have had. Instead, the emphasis gets placed on simply enforcing the rule.

This is why, no matter how often people are admonished to follow the rules, they never do. Control will be effective only when the rules are strictly enforced, but as soon as the control is relaxed, things will return to their earlier state. Managers sigh with frustration but resign themselves to the situation.

What they should be thinking about under these circumstances is whether it is the rules themselves or the work environment that makes the rules hard to follow. Instead of complaining about "no-good workers who can't follow the rules," these managers should be imagining ways to make the rules easier to follow.

In Japanese homes, people traditionally remove their shoes before entering, placing them in a line on the step. Once there was a mother who could never get her son to put his shoes in the right place, no matter how often she scolded him. The scolding, in fact, seemed to worsen the problem. In desperation, the mother marked the position of each shoe on the floor. The next day the boy, without being told, placed each shoe in its proper place. He continued to do this even after the marks wore off, for by then it had become a habit.

Another time a child could not distinguish between her left and right shoes and would often put them on backwards. No matter how often her parents showed her, she didn't understand the difference. It seemed that nothing could be done about it.

One day, someone had the idea to draw a cartoon face with half the face on each shoe; this created a sort of puzzle that would give her a model for the right way to put them on. After that, the child always put her shoes on the right way, and even placed them properly after taking them off.

The point is that a simple device can effectively solve a problem that was unvanquished by a hundred reprimands. Instead of complaining that our children are spoiled brats who never listen to us, we should come up with the right trick to make them listen.

The same is true of our workplace. When a problem persists no matter how many times it is pointed out, we need to come up with a device that will get proper attention.

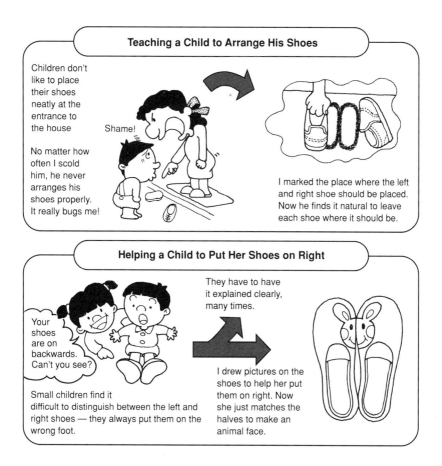

DISCUSSION QUESTIONS

What is the difference between hard work and resourcefulness?

Why is resourcefulness so important in today's business environment?

6

Kaizen Is Teaching People to Be Resourceful

LEARNING TO MAKE A HARD JOB EASIER

Ms. A, who recently joined a certain company, was assigned to final inspection of video products. The inspector hooks up samples of the video recorder and makes sure that the machine records and plays properly and that the color and sound meet standards. Each day, this person has to connect and disconnect the plugs of large connecting cords many times.

These plugs were very stiff. Since she had to connect and disconnect four plugs on each unit, Ms. A, who was not used to this operation, found this to be difficult work. It was especially hard on her hands, and her wrists and fingertips in particular ached.

It is a bitter experience when you can't get used to a job, even when you try hard. It's difficult to resist sighing and complaining to your supervisor and fellow workers. Some people will say, "Stop whining; you have to be patient." Some will be more comforting: "After a while, you'll get used to this, so just hang in there." Ms. A expected to hear this kind of advice in response to her complaints.

But the management at this company was not typical. One day the supervisor brought in a device that looked like a small rake and suggested she try using it to disconnect the plugs. Ms. A was surprised. Her manager did not scold her or even admonish her to work harder. Instead, the manager was teaching her how to change the method, asking "Why don't you try this?"

Although the tool looked terribly unprofessional, it made the plugging and unplugging operation a breeze. It was definitely more pleasant than trying to work harder despite the pain in her fingers. Moreover, it was much faster. Ms. A could now see the point of the kaizen activities that had been explained to her during her employee orientation.

But this is not the end of the story.

An Idea Inspires Other Ideas

After about a week had passed, Ms. A brought another tool to her supervisor's office. "Thank you for helping me out with the tool for pulling plugs the other day. My work is much more pleasant now. When I was using that tool, I thought of something to improve it."

Then she showed her tool. "Since there are four plugs, I made four notches in the rake instead of two. I also glued rubber on the steel plate to prevent it from scratching the product. Also, when I pull at the plugs, it works better if this part is in this angle. And finally, I made a notch here in the wooden handle, because that way it is easier to hold it in my hand."

Now it was supervisor's turn to be surprised. This employee had barely one week with the company, yet she was able to make a substantial improvement in her job. Her kaizen meant better performance, better efficiency, and better quality. "Well, this is a great kaizen. Please write it up right away so that we can submit it as an improvement proposal." She submitted the proposal and it won an award.

Ms. A was so pleased with this experience that she soon went on to devise other improvement proposals, all of which won her a prize as the "New Employee Kaizen Champion." By that point, Ms. A clearly had the knack of kaizen.

Resourcefulness Leads to Individual Development

What is the starting point for kaizen? In Ms. A's case, it was pain in her fingers.

Had she continued doing the job the way it was done before, she would have had to overcome the pain, and after a week or so she might have gotten used to it. But if she had gotten used to it, that would be the end of the story. There would be no need for kaizen. After a year or so, another employee would join the company and go through the same experience. And the same thing would be repeated time after time.

It may seem as though problems are solved when we get used to things, but in fact we just don't see them anymore. And since the problem has not been eliminated, it will reappear when a new employee is hired. When you work in a place where problems are "overcome" through simple perseverance and hard work, the problems won't go away, because nothing has been done to change the method.

Ms. A was fortunate to work in a place where work methods could be changed through resourcefulness. Thus problems can be solved at their source and true progress is possible. This is true no matter how small the improvement.

But the biggest benefit is really in the development of the people. What would be the situation if Ms. A were forced to "be patient"? No doubt the company would have gained one more patient employee — but that would have been the only benefit. The employee would have experienced no further professional growth whatsoever. Instead, she was encouraged to use her resourcefulness.

Proposal for a Plug-pulling Tool

Before improvement — After inspection of a video set, each plug had to be pulled by hand

Problem areas

1. Since removing the plugs takes force, your wrists and fingers hurt when you have to do it all day long.
2. That is why it also takes time to remove the plug.

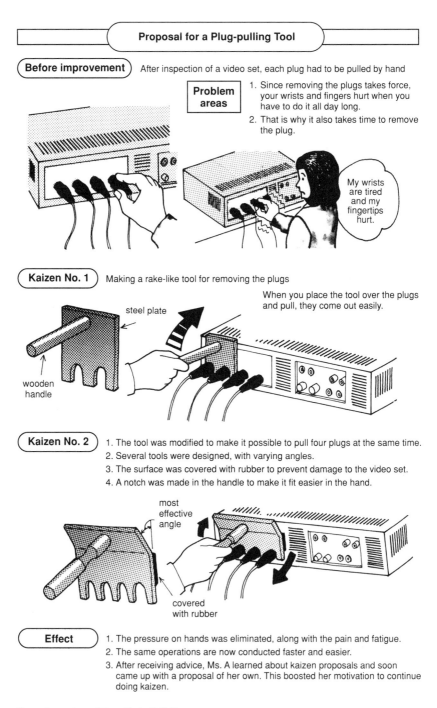

My wrists are tired and my fingertips hurt.

Kaizen No. 1 — Making a rake-like tool for removing the plugs

When you place the tool over the plugs and pull, they come out easily.

steel plate

wooden handle

Kaizen No. 2

1. The tool was modified to make it possible to pull four plugs at the same time.
2. Several tools were designed, with varying angles.
3. The surface was covered with rubber to prevent damage to the video set.
4. A notch was made in the handle to make it fit easier in the hand.

most effective angle

covered with rubber

Effect

1. The pressure on hands was eliminated, along with the pain and fatigue.
2. The same operations are now conducted faster and easier.
3. After receiving advice, Ms. A learned about kaizen proposals and soon came up with a proposal of her own. This boosted her motivation to continue doing kaizen.

Example courtesy of Sony Koda, K.K. Company

Once people have discovered the effectiveness of ingenuity, there will be no stopping them. They will progress to problems of increasing difficulty and actively improve their own jobs. During this process, they will aggressively acquire new skills, techniques, and knowledge.

A Policy that Promotes Ingenuity over Hard Work

Are people instinctively inclined toward one approach over the other? The answer depends on the atmosphere at their workplace — on how their problems are received by managers.

If the company policy is to stress hard work, the consequence will be that people stop trying to use their ingenuity. After that, only patience and perseverance will be left. But any place in which those are the only virtues is a wasteland where nothing will grow.

Of course, there are some problems that only hard work can overcome. If, for instance, a certain job must be finished by tomorrow, a person might have to work overtime if that's what it takes to get the job done.

Chances are, however, all you get is thanks for staying late to finish on time. What will happen next time? You'll most likely work all night again next month if the situation requires it. Nothing will have changed about the way this particular job is done. The same level of performance is repeated over and over again.

A zero will always be a zero. However, when you apply ingenuity, the improvement, no matter how small, will continuously compound. The total effect of each of these improvements can be very significant.

We will look at several case studies as examples of what can happen when workplace problems are solved through resourcefulness and ingenuity rather than hard work.

CASE STUDY 1: INGENUITY MEANS MISTAKE-PROOFING

A final step in speedometer assembly involves attaching a display panel to the meter. It is a simple operation, requiring only a few screws, but the screwdriver sometimes damages the display panel.

Every driver pays close attention to the speedometer. If the display panel is scratched, car buyers will assume that its function is compromised. Indeed, a scratch on something as basic as the speedometer might lead the buyer to question the quality of the entire car.

For this reason, assembly workers at a certain plant were extremely careful during this particular operation. In fact, their constant anxiety about the job gave them emotional distress and stiff shoulders, and their efficiency declined.

An innovative solution took the anxiety out of the job so that even if a worker's hand slipped, the screwdriver would not damage the display board. The device was a protective plastic cover put over the display board. Since the locations for the screws are predetermined, the screwdriver should contact the display board only in those locations. When small openings are made in the plastic cover above those locations, a worker can use the screwdriver without taking special care. The risk of scratching the display board is eliminated.

This looked like a final solution. It was made into an operating standard and the manager in charge of kaizen was greatly relieved. But although it looked like a great idea, it was not implemented the way it should have been.

As it turned out, the task of applying and removing the plastic cover proved to be just too much of a hassle. Experienced operators wouldn't bother with the device, feeling that they didn't really need it.

The person who came up with the idea was frustrated, but it was no use getting angry or telling the other workers to stick to the operating standards. Since she came up with the idea to take the anxiety out of the job, she had to take another step. She had to create a way to make it easy to follow the standard, rather than trying to force them to do it.

Once a person's perception changes, ideas come out easily. The solution was to make a cover that automatically came down when the operator picked up a screwdriver and raised itself when the operator released the screwdriver. Now the workers no longer have to make a conscious effort to follow the rules by moving the cover up and down. When they start work, the cover is already in place.

CASE STUDY 2: INGENUITY MEANS NOT BEING PATIENT

In computer assembly, the worker has to install a number of different electronic components on the circuit board. One of the components, called a dip switch, has eight terminals that must be set to the left or right. Each model has different specifications for which terminals to set. At one plant, the assembly worker had to count the terminals to determine which ones to set. If a single terminal was set in the wrong position, the computer would not work properly, and this would be a big problem.

The operation itself was simple. All a worker had to do was to push the terminal with a pair of tweezers. However, since the parts are so tiny, the operation made people nervous and was hard on their eyes. Even with patience and concentration, it was impossible not to make a mistake, and it took time to inspect for them. Operation efficiency, therefore, was low.

Even though the pattern for setting the terminal settings would vary according to the specifications for a given computer, it did not mean that each piece had a different specification. The same pattern would apply to several hundred units. Nevertheless, each terminal of each dip switch was set individually with one pair of tweezers.

Ms. B felt that what she was doing seemed like an immense waste of time. She wondered to herself, "Is it really

A Protective Cover for Attaching Display Panels

Before improvement

When attaching the display panel with a screwdriver, the workers would sometimes scratch it.

Kaizen No. 1

The panel was protected with a plastic cover that had openings only over the locations where the screws were to be attached.

Problem area: Some people still performed the operation without using the cover because it was a hassle for them to raise and lower the cover.

Kaizen No. 2

The plastic cover automatically came down over the panel when the worker picked up a screwdriver and raised when the screwdriver was released.

Effect

1. Scratches on the display panels have been eliminated.
2. Since no one has to deal with raising and lowering the cover now, this is a perfect solution.

Example courtesy of Kanto Seiki K.K. Company

necessary to set each terminal one by one, or could I use some method that would set all eight at the same time?"

How about using a tool to push over the terminals? At that point, the idea of a comb-like tool started taking shape in her mind. To be more precise, it looked like a comb with missing teeth. In places where there were teeth, the tool would push over the terminals; where there are no teeth, the position would not be changed. "That's it, it can be done with a comb with missing teeth! The tooth arrangement can be adjusted depending on the specifications of a given computer, and then it'll be a breeze."

She immediately made a device out of a small piece of acrylic, cutting out the proper shape with a utility knife. When she tried it out on a computer, it worked.

Once the initial arrangement of positions was correct (all terminals on one side), there was no way to make a mistake. The result was a perfect one-touch operation. Moreover, there was no need for inspection. The tool itself took care of the checking, so that the operation to set the terminals also served to verify the position of those terminals.

The starting point of Ms. B's kaizen was the recognition that the purpose of the terminal-setting operation was always to create the same pattern.

CASE STUDY 3: INGENUITY MEANS NOT HAVING TO WORK SO HARD

All human work can be divided into three general categories:

- Work that requires mainly physical effort
- Work that requires the use of our senses
- Work that requires use of our mental judgment

The machine age began with machines that were designed to reduce hard physical work and enhance human muscle power; these were tools such as hammers and levers.

An Ingenious Device for Setting Dip Switch Terminals

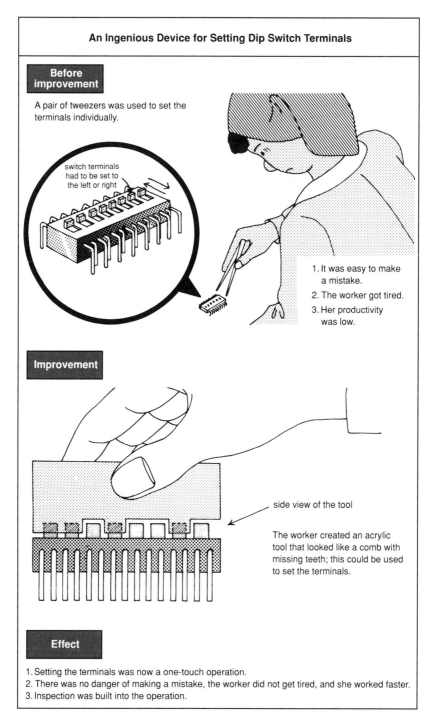

Before improvement

A pair of tweezers was used to set the terminals individually.

switch terminals had to be set to the left or right

1. It was easy to make a mistake.
2. The worker got tired.
3. Her productivity was low.

Improvement

side view of the tool

The worker created an acrylic tool that looked like a comb with missing teeth; this could be used to set the terminals.

Effect

1. Setting the terminals was now a one-touch operation.
2. There was no danger of making a mistake, the worker did not get tired, and she worked faster.
3. Inspection was built into the operation.

Example courtesy of Epson Co.

Powering these early machines were animals, wind, and water, among other elements. Today, with the availability of engines, humans have immense power at their disposal to carry out physical work.

The next step was the use of tools such as guides and sensors that replace human senses in conducting detailed measurements and making fine adjustments. Simple calculating operations also fit into this category.

The most recent step involves the development of devices that weigh information and make decisions, freeing people for other tasks. Artificial intelligence is an important product of this stage.

This macroscopic view of the stages of industrial history can also be applied to kaizen activities in the workplace. The first thing required is ingenuity to make hard physical work easier and safer.

At a certain company, for example, iron filings were mixed with grinding fluid during a grinding operation. The magnetic device for cleaning the filings out of the water was not entirely efficient, so employees had to manually dredge out the filings that sank to the bottom of the collecting tank. This operation was very inefficient. An obvious solution would be to get some mechanical device to do the job, perhaps a pump driven by an electric motor. However, such a common solution lacks ingenuity.

Electricity is not the only source of energy that can do work. The best idea in this case was a simple pump that used water pressure to remove the filings. When water from a high-pressure main is injected through a narrow nozzle into the pipe, the liquid around the nozzle also will be drawn up by suction. This way, iron filings gathered at the bottom will be pumped up along with the water. As this less saturated water flows back over the magnetic filing-removal device, the filings are collected without hard work.

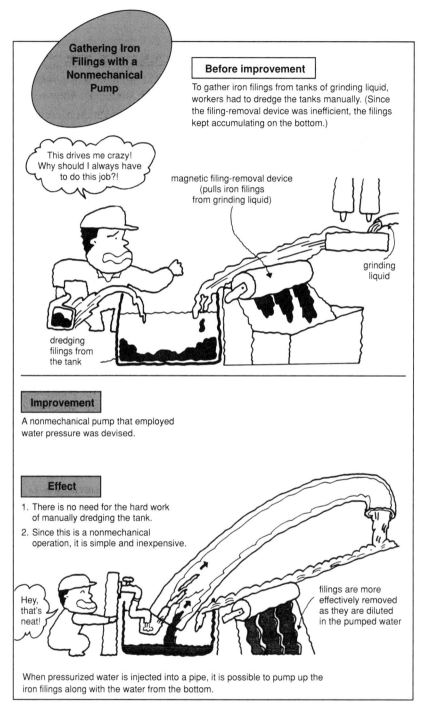

Gathering Iron Filings with a Nonmechanical Pump

Before improvement

To gather iron filings from tanks of grinding liquid, workers had to dredge the tanks manually. (Since the filing-removal device was inefficient, the filings kept accumulating on the bottom.)

This drives me crazy! Why should I always have to do this job?!

magnetic filing-removal device (pulls iron filings from grinding liquid)

grinding liquid

dredging filings from the tank

Improvement

A nonmechanical pump that employed water pressure was devised.

Effect

1. There is no need for the hard work of manually dredging the tank.
2. Since this is a nonmechanical operation, it is simple and inexpensive.

Hey, that's neat!

filings are more effectively removed as they are diluted in the pumped water

When pressurized water is injected into a pipe, it is possible to pump up the iron filings along with the water from the bottom.

Example courtesy of Iseki Noki Co.

DISCUSSION QUESTIONS

How does being resourceful affect employees?

How does being resourceful affect the job?

7

Kaizen Means Pursuing a Purpose

The starting point of every improvement is the question, "What is the purpose of this job? Why am I doing this?" When you start thinking along these lines, you are going in the right direction.

If the purpose of a job is not clear, people tend to pay too much attention to the *means* of doing it. They forget that there may be more than one way to get to the end result. This makes kaizen difficult, because there is always some way the job "has always been done." With the understanding that there are many means and that means can be changed, however, people start to consider whether there are better or easier ways.

WHY SWEEP THE RAILWAY STATIONS?

Although litter may not be a problem in train stations that have adopted electronic pass-reading systems, the floors of many stations in Japan are littered with small circles of paper, the waste from holes punched in tickets. These little bits of paper must be swept up by station employees.

In Nagoya, however, you won't see any waste lying around on the station floors. If you watch the activities there, you will notice that the conductors who punch tickets have small plastic canisters attached to the punchers. Those little bits of paper that would have to be swept later fall instead into the plastic case when punched out. This type of kaizen is based on eliminating the cause of an inconvenience. An operation that consisted of three steps — punching, scattering of bits of paper, and gathering them again (by cleaning) — has been replaced by a shorter operation consisting of only one step.

Let's look at the background and concept behind this kaizen. If kaizen, which is about changing methods of work, had not been promoted at this worksite, station employees would have continued dutifully to sweep the platform as if cleaning up the ticket holes was their mission.

But why do employees sweep up these little bits of paper? Is it because they are directed to do so, or because they want customers to have pleasant surroundings in the stations?

When cleaning itself becomes a purpose, employees will devote themselves to cleaning. Their supervisors may even praise them for being diligent workers. This approach was the trend ten years ago. Today, however, management efficiency is required, and we should no longer blindly praise such an attitude.

Hard work is appreciated. However, hard work based on a mistaken purpose is not appreciated, no matter how intensely performed. We have to recognize the purpose of the work that we do, and then we have to find ways of doing that job better.

That makes it less important to do the job as we are directed than to find different ways of doing the job through kaizen. That is why companies formulate kaizen proposal programs, award prizes for proposals, and encourage improvement activities.

SIMPLE IDEAS ARE THE BEST KAIZEN

The initial idea for dealing with the ticket-hole litter problem was to install an electronic pass-reading system and do

The Problem of Ticket Holes

Before improvement
Little circles of paper were scattered everywhere and had to be swept up.

Improvement
Why not gather the punched holes before they fall to the ground?

a plastic canister

• The best improvement would be to make sure no paper circles fall down after punching. That is the aim of this kaizen.

Example courtesy of Nagoya Railroad.

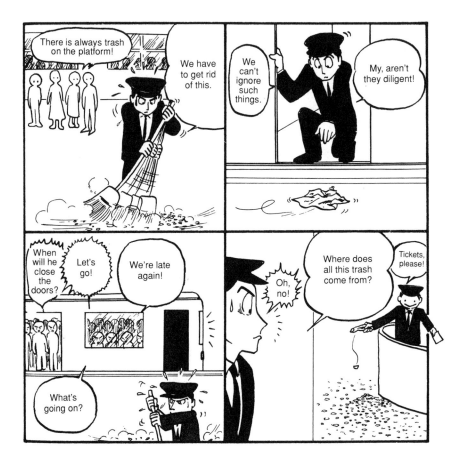

away with ticket punching. This is an ambitious idea. Unfortunately, to implement it the company would need to make a large investment in new equipment or rewrite regulations. Moreover, the idea involves complex technological problems that are best left to the expertise of the technical departments.

Things being as they are, the next best thing would be kaizen ideas that people can implement in their own areas of responsibility, such as improvement of the dustpans or brooms.

One idea was to create a robot to sweep the station automatically — a real masterpiece of creative imagination.

The proposals for improving the cleaning tools probably received great praise. They deserved recognition since they were implemented by the people who proposed them. Certainly, their attitude is more positive than that of employees who make grandiose proposals and then grumble when the company doesn't accept them. But such small scale ideas should not be received uncritically. These, for example, still bought into the assumption that the purpose of the employees' job was to clean the station. They took only one step toward kaizen; stopping there would mean that they could never achieve real kaizen. Real kaizen means pursuit of better means to carry out the *purpose* of the job.

In this case, the purpose of the station employees' job was not to clean the station but to keep the station tidy and pleasant. Cleaning was just one of the means available to do the job. A better method would be one that eliminated the need for cleaning altogether.

USING KAIZEN TO ATTACK THE HEART OF THE PROBLEM

When comparing an automated cleaning machine with a little plastic canister, we might be tempted to praise the automated device. We might even laugh at the plastic canisters. But that response would be a mistake, and one based on a misunderstanding of kaizen.

A genuine kaizen improvement tends to be very simple. The more we find out about the details of the problems in our own jobs, the simpler and more effective our kaizen ideas become. An idea whose complexity dazzles is often only the superficial pursuit of a false purpose. No matter how wonderful the cleaning robot, it is inferior to a device that achieves the purpose by eliminating the need for cleaning.

Super Robo-Cleaner

**What's this?
You just attached a
plastic canister
to collect the
punched-out circles?**

Electronic
passreaders

A small plastic canister

THE BEST KAIZEN FINDS THE SHORTEST WAY TO ACCOMPLISH THE PURPOSE

Let us briefly summarize what we know about kaizen.

1. There are a number of paths to achievement of our purpose.
2. The methods we are accustomed to often no longer apply to conditions of the present era.
3. Kaizen means seeking better methods in accordance with the requirements of the actual situation.

4. The best kaizen is finding the simplest way to achieve the purpose of the job, simplifying the methods and means that we are using.

5. A poor kaizen idea is a detour around the true purpose of the work. It makes the methods more complicated.

6. An idea that achieves tremendous efficiency but requires considerable investment and a restructuring of the whole system is an innovation or breakthrough. Such innovations exceed the scope of kaizen and are difficult for the average employee to implement.

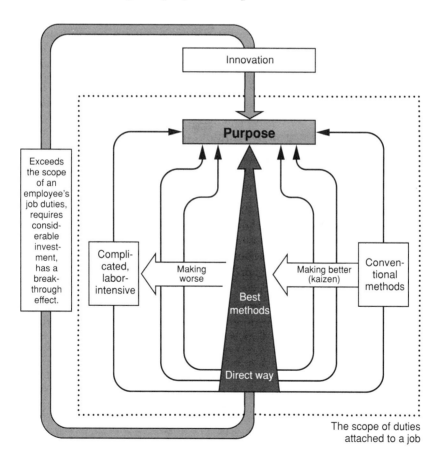

DISCUSSION QUESTION

In the example of the railway station litter, why was the idea to attach a canister to the ticket punchers superior to the one to create a robotic sweeper?

(Answer: The canister solution addressed the true purpose of the station employees' jobs, which was to keep the station tidy and pleasant. Thus, it eliminated the need for sweeping.)

8

Kaizen Requires a Transfer of Know-how

AN EFFICIENT WAY TO IMPROVE GIFT-WRAPPING

The illustration on page 77 shows a scene at the gift-wrapping counter in a department store. Gift wrapping is difficult for inexperienced employees. Customers served by new employees often must wait a long time, after which they receive a poorly wrapped package. It is no wonder customers complained about this problem.

During the busiest gift-giving seasons, the department store hired students and other part-time workers to help out. But when these employees were put in charge of gift wrapping, this service would deteriorate. The problem caused constant headaches for the store managers, and it was repeated every year, without exception.

Since the situation was bad in every store, the store managers had simply resigned themselves to it. If this attitude prevailed, the employees would soon think that way about all the problems they encountered. Before long, the store would acquire a bad reputation and lose customers.

"We must not inconvenience our customers. Isn't there a clever way to solve this problem?" "Maybe they do this in other stores, but in *our* store, shouldn't there be a better way?" The people who thought along these lines knew that this problem simply must be solved. That's the way kaizen usually starts.

Looking for Another Way to Do the Job

Some kaizen practices implemented in other stores to address this problem included:

- training sessions or gift-wrapping classes to teach special skills and provide necessary practice
- standardization of wrapping methods, instruction manuals, etc.

When the company approached its own workers for better ideas, they suggested:

- wrapping standard articles beforehand
- replacing gift wrap with attractive gift bags

Without question, these solutions represent kaizen proposals. They suggest countermeasures to the cause of the problem. Specifically, they deal with the problem in the following ways:

- People don't like to wait long for the gift to be wrapped. Pre-wrapping would eliminate any waiting.
- Messy wrapping looks unattractive. The problem would be solved if the store used gift bags instead of wrap.

These are logical conclusions. But whether we can apply them easily to existing conditions is another thing. The things that customers buy come in different sizes. Even the standard boxes that this store provides for gifts come in six different sizes. And when the employees try to use gift bags, many customers tell them that a bag is not appropriate for their particular gift and insist on gift wrapping.

The Root Cause of the Problem: Lack of Know-how

Does anyone have a better idea? In thinking about a proposal, one that goes to the very heart of the problem, we have to return to the principles of kaizen and pursue the actual causes of the inconvenience.

If we ask the question "why is the wrapping so clumsy?" we might at first get an answer like the following: "because the employees are not used to doing it" or "because they are inexperienced." Since it must deal with the cause, the proposed countermeasure might be to "get them used to it" or "give them more experience." These measures would require holding special training sessions, lectures, and demonstrations.

But are unfamiliarity and lack of experience the real causes of the problem? If that were the case, then special training would be the only sensible countermeasure. Because training takes time, the store would be unable to overcome its problems quickly.

If you are serious about kaizen, you must go one step further in pursuing the real causes. You must ask yourself *why* again. Why does inexperience cause people to wrap so clumsily? Why do they become experts once they get used to doing it properly? You will then understand what is causing inexperienced wrappers to make mistakes and waste time.

Observe how the job is being done. What are the main components of the operation? One of them is to select the size of the sheet of wrapping paper by looking at the size of the customer's gift. Experienced employees can take one look and determine immediately what size of paper to use. Novices start messing things up from this moment. Once they reach for a piece of paper that is too big or too small, the final result will always be sloppy. If there was a method to determine the right size of paper that even inexperienced employees could use, this might take care of a big problem.

The other point is to determine how to position the box on the wrapping paper. Here again, experienced wrappers can determine the best position at a glance. Inexperienced wrappers sometimes put the box in the middle of the paper, and sometimes closer to the edges, making an end product that is bulky or leaves corners uncovered. If there were a way to take the guesswork out of this component of the operation, this problem too might be solved.

Once we understand the relation between the way a certain job is performed and where the problems lie, we will be able to see the measures that can be taken. We could, for instance, create sample boxes with corresponding paper sizes, or create marks and creases on the paper.

After experimentation with several similar proposals, a wonderful idea was born: create templates for positioning the boxes on the paper.

A Solution that Makes Everyone an Expert

A set of six cardboard templates was created, corresponding to the standard box sizes. The employee would select the right size by matching the edge of one of the templates with the longest side of the box. The employee would then read the paper size number written on the matching template, and thus would always reach for the right size of paper.

Using this method, even new employees were able to determine the right size of paper without delay. All they had to do was match the box with a template.

Next, the right angle of the template is fitted over one corner of the paper, and the box is placed on the paper along the diagonal side of the template. When the template is lifted, the box is positioned for wrapping. Using this method, anyone can deliver a perfect wrapping job. There is no longer any need to "get used to" the operation or to puzzle over where to place the box. There is no risk of making a mistake.

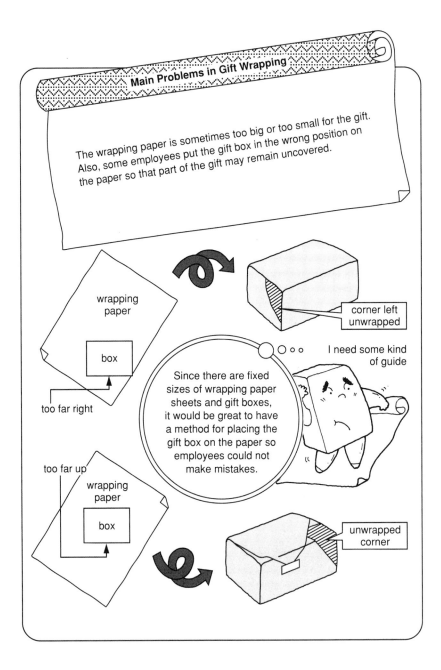

Main Problems in Gift Wrapping

The wrapping paper is sometimes too big or too small for the gift. Also, some employees put the gift box in the wrong position on the paper so that part of the gift may remain uncovered.

wrapping paper

corner left unwrapped

box

too far right

I need some kind of guide

Since there are fixed sizes of wrapping paper sheets and gift boxes, it would be great to have a method for placing the gift box on the paper so employees could not make mistakes.

too far up

wrapping paper

box

unwrapped corner

It was no longer necessary to hold special training sessions. Through a half dozen cardboard templates, gift-wrapping know-how was transferred from experienced employees to inexperienced employees. Now no one needed time to "get used to" the job.

On the other hand, it does not look good when employees have to reach for a template every time they wrap something, which is why the store is also conducting gift-wrapping training sessions. But with the templates, the training takes one-quarter of the time previously required. Now there is little difference between people who are skillful with their fingers and those who are not.

In contrast to the conventional training of watching and imitating senior employees and teachers, the templates make it easy to learn the elements of gift wrapping. The company uses durable acrylic templates, which are available to employees in all of its stores.

MULTIPLE CAUSES: NO LONGER A STUMBLING BLOCK

If the only cause of the employees' clumsiness at gift wrapping was that they hadn't practiced it long enough, the appropriate countermeasure would be to provide exposure so that employees would get used to it. Special training sessions and lectures would be necessary.

Upon analysis of the operation, however, we see that it consists of two main components — knowing the size of the paper to use and the position where the box should be placed. Understanding these elements provided the clues for developing a kaizen proposal to help workers grasp the proper method quickly.

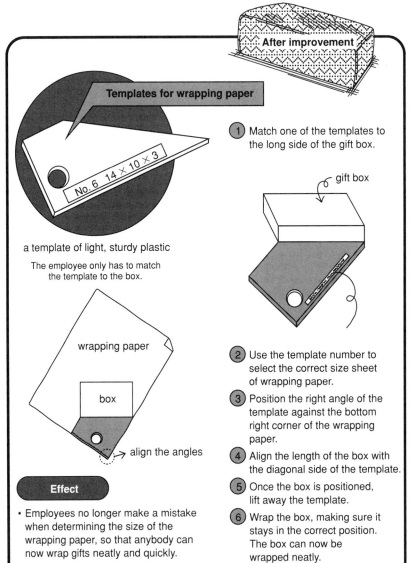

After improvement

Templates for wrapping paper

No. 6 14 × 10 × 3

a template of light, sturdy plastic

The employee only has to match
the template to the box.

wrapping paper

box

align the angles

Effect

• Employees no longer make a mistake
when determining the size of the
wrapping paper, so that anybody can
now wrap gifts neatly and quickly.
• Customer waiting times were shortened.

(1) Match one of the templates to
the long side of the gift box.

gift box

(2) Use the template number to
select the correct size sheet
of wrapping paper.

(3) Position the right angle of the
template against the bottom
right corner of the wrapping
paper.

(4) Align the length of the box with
the diagonal side of the template.

(5) Once the box is positioned,
lift away the template.

(6) Wrap the box, making sure it
stays in the correct position.
The box can now be
wrapped neatly.

Example provided courtesy of Nichii Co.

Multiple Countermeasures for Multiple Causes

An analysis of a problem often reveals that it has more than one primary cause. People who assume that every problem has a single cause often come up with only one cause, and therefore propose only one countermeasure.

It sometimes happens that a single countermeasure is indeed all that is needed. If only one is proposed when more are needed, however, the proposal is apt to stall. Then the proposer will complain that the company is ignoring his or her idea.

But people who allow for the possibility that a problem can have multiple causes hardly ever hit such a stumbling block, because they are able to propose a number of countermeasures.

People should not get discouraged when one particular idea is not accepted to remedy a certain situation. They can prepare a number of alternative proposals and suggest another idea instead. If there is a broad range of proposals to choose from, the proposal selected is likely to be the most effective, the easiest to implement, the least expensive, and the least labor-intensive. That is the goal of kaizen proposal activities.

People who have mastered kaizen do not necessarily have special skills or talents. The ideas that are implemented are not extraordinary concepts. More often than not, the commonsense solution is the one chosen, the one even a conservative supervisor can understand.

What these people do have is the flexibility to come up with multiple ideas. Their adaptability is based on the ability to view things from several angles.

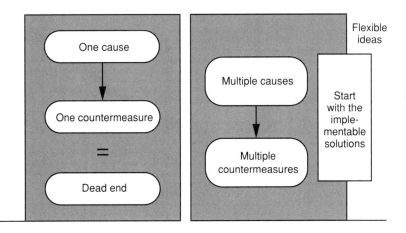

EFFECTIVE KAIZEN DEALS WITH THE CAUSES OF PROBLEMS

Every situation, no matter how complex it may seem, can be broken down into separate components. Once you analyze a problem's main components, its true nature becomes apparent, as do the countermeasures and methods that can solve the problem. If you neglect this step, you cannot reach the heart of the problem.

It is easy to jump to the wrong conclusion when we miss the big picture. We blame problems on how busy, hurried, or inexperienced we are. Thus the countermeasures we devise are equally superficial.

Employees often get the feedback that their proposal is unacceptable because it is not a "fundamental solution." Of course, a fundamental solution is ideal. But in kaizen activity, managers should not necessarily require fundamental solutions immediately. If a proposal eliminates some causes and disposes of the inconvenience, it must be considered a good proposal.

After all, partially eliminated problems represent a certain progress. As they delve into the problem further, however, employees should grapple with more important causes of problems and thus achieve greater efficiency.

DISCUSSION QUESTIONS

In the example of the poor gift-wrapping service, why was the idea to use templates superior to a call for special training sessions?

Why is it important to come up with multiple countermeasures to a problem?

9

Kaizen Means Knowing When to Eliminate, Reduce, or Change an Activity

Masayasu Tanaka tells the following story in his book, *VE* (published in Japan by Management). It describes the plant of a manufacturer of steamed dumplings, called *manju* in Japanese. All the steps required to make the dumplings have been automated, except one final step — making a twist on top of the dumpling.

This twist had to be formed by hand, which of course meant that the plant's productivity was low. One day the president of the company called a meeting of the engineers and instructed them to automate the entire manufacturing process. Having to develop a machine that puts a twist on a dumpling is not something that makes an engineer flush with pride. Nevertheless, after many sleepless nights, much research, and many trial productions and experiments, workers built a machine that would automatically add the twist on top.

There was joy and jubilation in the plant. "Finally, we have automated all the steps of the manufacturing process." In the midst of this atmosphere of delight over the birth of sophisticated equipment, someone quietly asked, "What is this twist for, anyway?"

These words suddenly revealed the pointlessness of the engineers' hardships.

Why a Twist?

The engineers who had worked so hard to develop the automatic dimple machine shook their heads, groping for answer. "That's a good question — what *is* it for?" No one seemed to know the reason for the twist.

After thorough investigation, they discovered that the twist was added to distinguish meat dumplings from sweet

What Is the Twist for?

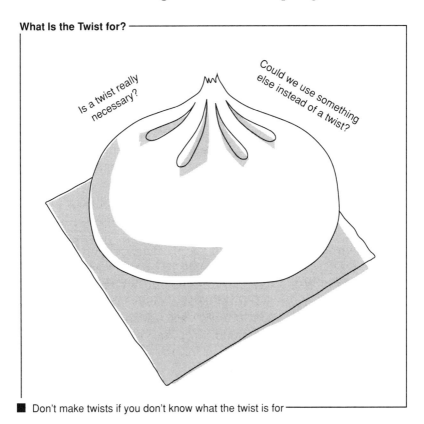

■ Don't make twists if you don't know what the twist is for

dumplings. But a twist is not the only way to make this distinction. Other methods might include

- making a dent or cut
- adding color
- stamping a pattern
- using different color for the paper and packaging

With these methods, full automation would be simple. There would be no need for great effort and expense to automate the twisting process.

In the old days, when meat dumplings were made by hand, putting a twist on each one was the most effective way to distinguish them from the sweet dumplings. The workers had only to make a small movement with their fingers.

But just because this used to be the best way doesn't mean that it is still the best way. As machines start doing work that used to be done manually, the way we do our jobs necessarily changes. In this case, making a twist might be the worst possible way to distinguish the dumplings.

Focus on the Purpose

Instead of asking themselves how they could automate the twist making, the engineers should have first posed the question, "What is the purpose of the twist?" Had they done so, they could have spared themselves a great deal of useless trouble.

When we focus on the ultimate purpose of an activity, we can come up with a number of ways to accomplish that purpose. Consequently, we can select the simplest and most efficient method. If we reverse the emphasis and instead ask "What is the best way of doing this?" the means we develop is likely to be useless. Without the big picture, we stray into one-sided concepts.

Elimination May Be the Best Improvement

Once we have established the purpose of an activity, our next step is to devise an improvement. So our natural inclination is to come up with another activity that improves the original one. But this approach ignores a basic principle of kaizen, which is the principle of *elimination*.

Before considering other options, consider whether you can drop the activity altogether. Eliminating an activity rarely requires great ingenuity; often, it is the most effective and least expensive improvement there is.

When we start thinking in terms of eliminating an activity, the question that naturally arises is, "Is it okay to drop it?" This question inevitably leads you to ask, "What is the purpose of what I am doing?"

If we ponder what would happen should a certain activity be eliminated, we often realize that nothing would happen. Something that might have been necessary before, like twists in dumplings, may now be obsolete. In such cases, elimination is the best improvement.

Unfortunately, we sometimes fail to notice this. Most of the time, we live with things as they are simply because it's the way we've always done it, the way we were taught. Elimination is a key concept that presumes awareness of the real condition of things. When we ask, "Wouldn't it be just as well to eliminate this?" we are in fact questioning whether the way we do our job makes sense.

The answer we get is either "I can't eliminate this, as much as I would like to," or "I can drop it and nothing will happen." In other words, we determine which methods are essential to the job and which are not.

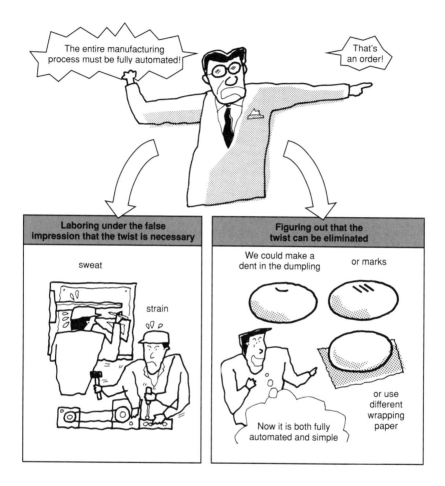

ELIMINATION IS THE ULTIMATE KAIZEN

The inventory control process at one company involved validating paper inventory slips by stamping them with a personal seal. The employees had done this for so long that they had forgotten why it was necessary, until one day a new worker asked, "Do we really need to do this?"

Originally, employees affixed their personal seals to various documents circulating in the company to indicate what was authorized by whom. At that time, since all the vouchers processed had to be written by hand, affixing a personal seal to the documents was necessary for determining who was in charge of what, who checked, and who authorized it.

Today, however, the number of each operator and checker is registered automatically, making it clear where the responsibility lies. Therefore, the question arose whether the old system of validating everything with personal seals was still necessary.

After the matter was examined, the proposed approach was adopted promptly. Affixing personal seals to documents meant processing work on a large number of documents each day, which made no sense. By eliminating this operation, the productivity of the output was raised significantly.

This proposal simply questioned the logic of "doing things the way we were told to." It asked, "What is the purpose of stamping the seals?" In so doing, it eliminated useless work that hampered productivity.

As times change, things that used to be necessary to do a job properly sometimes lose their meaning. This often causes unexpected problems. When people go about a job without giving it much thought, they may continue doing useless work without knowing it.

Taking a Fresh Look at How We Work

When one company ran a proposal campaign to flush out unnecessary activities in the workplace, employees came up with more than one hundred procedures and documents that were not needed. The company discovered that although its employees were often very busy, their work was not creating added value.

We shouldn't kid ourselves that this only happens to other companies. Do we always ask ourselves whether what we usually do in our jobs is really necessary to get the work done? If we don't, it is likely that at least some of the work we do has no meaning.

Our world is in a constant flux. That is why it is so important to stay focused on the purpose of our jobs and continually seek better ways to accomplish that purpose. In such a rapidly changing environment, elimination is the simplest kaizen and yet also the ultimate kaizen.

IF YOU CAN'T ELIMINATE, REDUCE THE NUMBER OF STEPS

Although elimination is the best kaizen, it is not always possible to simply abandon an entire operation. To use the example of the dumpling, if the twists had become a famous trademark of the company, it would have been unwise to stop creating them, because of the possible effect on sales. Moreover, a "simple" solution might not work if it creates legal problems or violates industrial regulations.

In such instances, we look to another principle of kaizen: *reduction*.

Combining Two Steps in One

The basic principle of reducing can be seen in many examples of kaizen proposals. An operation at one plant consisted of two steps: drilling holes with a narrow bit and beveling the hole edges with a larger bit. The first improvement proposed was to do away with the beveling step because, after all, elimination is the best kaizen.

In this case, however, the beveling was necessary for the required quality of the finishing. Therefore, the workers went on to the next improvement approach, which was to reduce the number of steps. After studying various methods, they came up with the idea to use a two-part bit, shown in the illustration.

With this bit, workers were able to bevel the opening at the same time they drilled the narrow hole. Since it was no longer necessary to change the bit and to determine the best position for finishing, this improvement significantly reduced the time required.

Example courtesy of Tohoku Oki Denki

Using Ingenuity to Reduce Strenuous and Repetitive Operations

Reduction is perhaps the most common feature of innovative proposals. We should particularly consider ways to reduce unpleasant jobs and strenuous operations.

Repetitive operations, in which workers have to do the same thing again and again, present one of the best targets for kaizen. Repeated rewriting of documents is a particularly unpleasant operation. It cries out for a quicker method of transferring information.

At one company, there was an operation that required workers to bend their backs and lift a heavy workpiece many times a day, every day. A proposal was made after someone wondered whether there was some way to lighten this burden.

Of course, the perfect kaizen would be to automate the operation so that people were no longer involved in transporting these workpieces. But such a complicated step would have been difficult to implement. The next best thing would be to eliminate the most strenuous operation. It was from this perspective that the proposal arose.

The proposal was to employ a device that works like a seesaw. When a part comes down the chute, its weight tips the bottom of the seesaw, raising it automatically. The workers no longer have to strain their backs lifting the part off the chute. Needless to say, the efficiency of the operation is greatly increased.

IF YOU CAN'T REDUCE, CHANGE SOMETHING

Unfortunately, we cannot solve every problem by eliminating an activity, or even by reducing the number of steps. What do we do then?

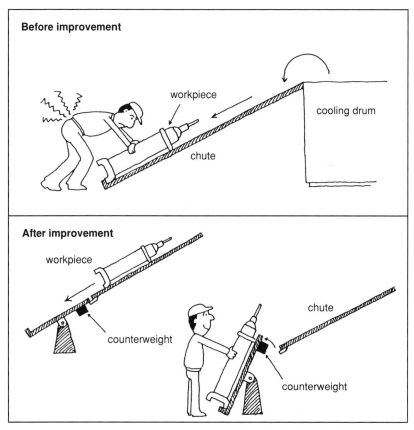

Before improvement

workpiece

cooling drum

chute

After improvement

workpiece

counterweight

chute

counterweight

Example courtesy of Toyota Motor Co.

Another principle of kaizen is *change*. A thesaurus lists several words that have the same meaning as *change*, including *replace, modify*, and *convert*. We can, for instance, change the sequence of an operation, replace a part with something else, change the quality, or modify the form. Clearly, there are many ways to change things.

We will not be able to change the situation unless we change some element of it. Of course, if we can change the essential elements of a situation, the effect will be tremendous. If that is not possible, however, changing other elements will bring some benefits.

Changing Equipment Position to Lighten the Work

The picture on page 98 is a good illustration of what can be achieved by a kaizen idea involving a simple change. Previously, it was necessary to hoist heavy pipes onto a raised scale platform to weigh them. Two workers had to exert a lot of effort during this operation. The workers wondered whether a change in things might relieve them of this effort.

Thus, a proposal was made to change the position of the scale. The scale was lowered into a recess in the floor so that the platform was level with the floor height. As a result, the same operation could be done by one worker and with much less exertion.

All that changed in this case was the position of the scale. It was not necessary to replace anything or use complicated equipment. A tremendous effect often can be achieved simply by changing a minor detail. We will explore this subject further in the following example.

Changing Round to Triangular Solves a Problem

The case in question involves a closing clamp whose function was to seal the lid of a plastic bucket used to transport the company's product. For some reason, this clamping mechanism didn't serve the function it was meant for. Many people complained that the lid easily came off. For instance, when buckets of product were transported by truck, vibrations loosened the clamps and the lid slipped off.

In due course, an inspector determined that the clamps were too loose and ordered them to be replaced with stiffer ones. From that point on, only stiff clamps were shipped.

Example from Japan Human Relations Association, ed., *The Idea Book: Improvement through TEI (Total Employee Involvement)* (Cambridge, Mass.: Productivity Press, 1988).

But when winter rolled around, new complaints started coming in. This time people complained that the clamp was so stiff it was hard to open the lid. Because it was cold, the drivers' hands were stiff, and since they wore work gloves, their hands would slip on the toggles of the clamp so that they could not open the lid at all.

The inspector racked his brains again. "First they complain that it comes off too easily, next they complain that it can't be opened. What am I supposed to do?"

The company had to take quick action to avoid losing customers. Customer complaints are a perfect opportunity to practice kaizen, provided that kaizen has taken root in the company culture.

Soon the company started soliciting employee ideas on the kind of change to make. Many ideas were submitted. Employees suggested

- replacing the clamping device with some other device
- clamping the lid with screws
- fastening the lid with a strap
- using a ratchet and quick-release method

These and other methods were proposed, but not one was implemented, because they lacked concrete designs.

Those ideas that stuck with the existing method of clamping the lid suggested changes such as

- moving the direction of the closing forward
- using elastic material for the arm of the clamp
- providing the clamp with a catch
- changing the shape of the toggle on the clamp

After much internal struggle, the company decided to change the toggle from a round shape to a triangular shape. Changing the shape would cost little, it did not involve a substantial design change, and it did not require significant modification of existing equipment. On top of that, it had a dramatic effect.

When a triangular toggle was used, the area of contact between the toggle and the lid was much larger, forming a plane rather than a single line. The new toggles kept the lids on, even through a lot of vibration.

The triangular shape of the toggle was easier to grab hold of. The round toggles had no place for fingers to grab; when drivers wore gloves, their fingers slipped and they could not release the clamps. With the triangular toggles, the drivers can release the lid even when they are wearing gloves.

The problem of the stiff clamp was solved by simply changing the shape of the toggle.

The company could have switched to another mechanism to seal the bucket lids, and in fact it seriously considered this alternative. But because it focused on what should be changed and how to change it, it avoided jumping to the wrong conclusion and was able to select the simplest and most effective improvement.

SUMMARY

Of the many principles of kaizen, these three are the most important:

- Eliminate the whole activity.
- Reduce the steps of the activity.
- Change the activity.

These three rules represent a formula that applies to all kaizen activity. Always consider whether the first principle can be followed before proceeding to the other two.

DISCUSSION QUESTIONS

Name the three types of kaizen activity, beginning with the most basic.

Design of a Closing Clamp

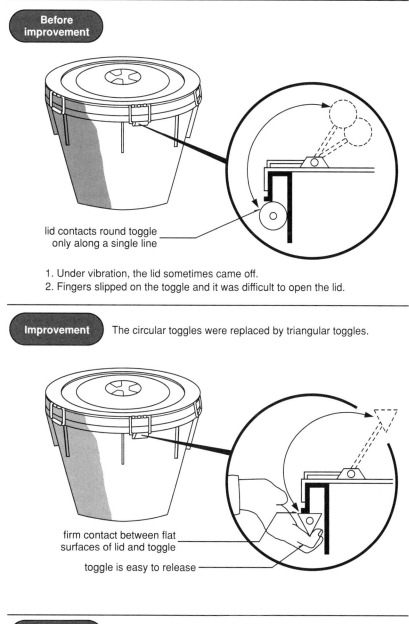

PART THREE

Providing Guidance for Kaizen Teian Activities — Principles and Rules

Teian is a system for educating employees through kaizen activities in the form of improvement proposals. This is why guidance from supervisors and communication between managers and those working for them are indispensable.

A kaizen teian (continuous improvement proposal) system has three important functions that will be addressed in the next chapters:

- Teian is designed to promote personal growth of employees as well as organizational growth.
- Teian represents an opportunity to provide guidance for employees.
- Teian serves as a barometer of leadership.

10

Teian Is Helping People and the Organization Grow Together

IS KAIZEN ACTIVITY TOO SLOW?

If our main purpose in proposal activities were to get results, it would be quickest to seek out the opinion of the top experts in a given field. An amateur's ability is usually far behind that of an expert or a knowledgeable consultant.

When amateurs try to innovate...

Promoting suggestion activity in a company is often a sluggish process — good ideas are few and far between. Most suggestions, if subjected to expert scrutiny, probably would be considered low-level ideas and wouldn't get far. They are just demands and complaints, not suggestions.

Supervisors and suggestion reviewers understandably get frustrated with a system that emphasizes results. A badly conceived suggestion system takes a lot of work, time, and money; in the end it becomes a game played for no good reason.

Many companies are now adopting kaizen teian (improvement proposal) systems. Some of these systems began more than 30 years ago and are still flourishing. Proposal systems have spread from manufacturing to sales, service, and banking.

There are two good reasons for having a proposal system. First, kaizen proposal activity brings results that are valuable to the company. Second, kaizen enhances the company by vitalizing the organization, developing individual abilities, and training human resources.

CONTINUOUS IMPROVEMENT OF MOTIVATION AND ABILITIES

If effects are all we are pursuing, it is more efficient to leave improvements up to the experts rather than to encourage them in bottom-up activities. However, leaving improvement to the professionals has some pitfalls.

1. It does not motivate other people to do kaizen, nor does it cultivate their abilities.
2. Although large-scale improvement proposals are implemented successfully, no attention is paid to the many small improvement ideas.
3. Ideas that might lead to labor efficiency or cost reduction are eagerly pursued, even though they might not be to the benefit of employees.

Improvements made by professionals (whether from inside or outside the organization) tend to lack continuity and durability because they do not utilize employees' kaizen abilities. This situation erodes employee motivation; people will do what they are ordered to do and nothing more. Thus employee motivation deteriorates even further.

If improvements require sophisticated, high-tech solutions, technical experts of course must be involved. However, they shouldn't be relied on for every small problem that arises.

In the old days, when mass production involved only a few product lines in each company, it was enough to rely on technical experts to make improvements. One improvement would remain effective for a long time.

Today, the old approach is not adequate when a wide range of small product quantities must be manufactured, revolutionary technologies are introduced quickly, and products are diversified right on the production line. The only way to achieve success is to take advantage of the knowledge and skills of those who work on the front lines.

The knowledge and information of those who actually do the work must be brought into the daily work. A kaizen teian system is nothing but a systematic organization of this activity.

PARTICIPATION IN KAIZEN IMPROVES WORK MORALE

Since kaizen is done by those who work at a job every day, it is only natural that its first target is inconveniences — things that make the work unpleasant, inexpedient, and unsafe.

The benefits gained by the improvement of working conditions is why the kaizen movement grows every year. Moreover, if improvements are made resourcefully, they do not conflict with productivity or quality improvement efforts. The differences between the top-down and bottom-up approaches to improvement can be summarized as follows.

Experts tend to concentrate on improvement that is visible and measurable. This is understandable, since the results must be exhibited as great achievements if the experts are to maintain their professional status.

Every workplace holds the seeds of many kaizen proposals

Improvements by professionals do not reflect the knowledge of people who are closest to the work. Furthermore, the new standards and methods are issued as orders. It is impossible to display the full potential of kaizen if people are simply expected to follow orders. Under such circumstances, employees have no incentive to come up with good ideas.

People naturally tend to resist ideas that are forced upon them and take ownership of ideas they help develop. Able to implement their own ideas, people become highly motivated.

There is no question that kaizen proposals and ideas that originate with employees are often unorganized. This is where the role of administrators and specialists comes in. It is their job to adjust, summarize, and make systematic use of improvement ideas from employees.

The effect of a single improvement may be small. But when each employee makes such improvements continuously, the cumulative effect is tremendous.

Managers sometimes think that a system will go out of control with too many incoming proposals. They shouldn't be afraid of that, however, because it reveals that all the employees are motivated. It is proof that the workplace is energized and the organization is working at full speed.

Directions and guidance should be provided not only for adjustments after an improvement, but also during the promotion of kaizen teian activities. It is important to clarify problems and point people's efforts in the right direction.

EDUCATING EMPLOYEES TO BE "SMART MISSILES"

In old-style naval battles, ships required a lot of ammunition to hit their targets. The commanding officer would watch the enemy ship and give orders to move the cannon to the right, forward, and so on. After several corrections, the gunners would shoot, and the cannonball *might* strike the enemy target.

The cannonballs went where you sent them; the problem was that often the target moved. After the commander fired, it was impossible to change the path of the cannonballs. Success depended on the commander's good coordination and clear perception of the situation. Even if these qualities were present, the efficiency of this type of warfare was poor.

Battles are fought differently these days. Instead of shooting cannonballs that fly only in the direction they were aimed, ships deploy missiles equipped with devices that detect the distance between the missile and the target. Such missiles can self-correct their course in accordance with directions received *after* they are launched.

Our job objectives are not so different — we too are trying to hit a moving target. To achieve this objective we must be capable of independent action. If our target makes complicated escape maneuvers, we must become like smart missiles, changing our course of action to meet those maneuvers.

As our environment becomes increasingly complicated and diversified, corporations have no choice but to achieve their objectives more efficiently. They need employees who

1. are aware of what and where the target is
2. can register the gap between the actual position and the target
3. can independently conceive and implement methods to reduce the gap
4. can correct their path to hit the target

In other words, companies today need employees who are like smart missiles. The cannonball type of employee cannot cope with changes and diversified situations. The missile type can hit the part of the target that will give the best results. A direct hit on the crux of the problem is the most effective way of doing one's job.

TEIAN MEANS INVESTMENT IN PEOPLE AND ADAPTABILITY TO CHANGES

Kaizen teian is geared to companies that use the missile approach to problem solving. Corporations that strive to develop a modern business strategy make an effort to train their employees as if they were their arsenal of missiles.

Clearly, such companies consider kaizen proposals a good investment in human resources and a natural part of job training. This seriousness shows in their efforts to promote the pro-

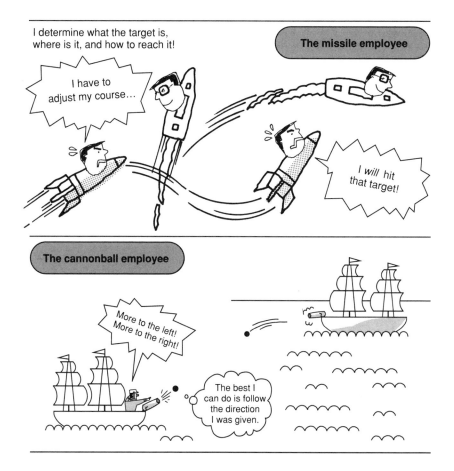

posal system and small group activities. Daily participation in an implemented proposal system, in which people identify their own problems and make improvements themselves, is part of the training for "smart-missile" employees.

This kind of education cannot be taught in classrooms; it involves skills that can be learned only on the job, in real practice. It is impossible to teach kaizen by having managers and supervisors preach its principles. What counts here is personal experience. Changing the way their jobs are done teaches employees and expands their perceptions of themselves. Proposal activity should provide continuous opportunities for practice; it develops capable employees on an ongoing basis.

Turning Inattentive Employees into Attentive Employees

To understand how to develop "smart-missile" employees, let's consider how employees might react to a problem like the following.

- A nail is sticking out.
- A machine makes a clattering noise.
- Mail comes back stamped "no such address."
- We have miscommunicated some news.
- Product sales are slow.

One employee takes no notice of the problem. When another person points it out, he might say, "I never thought about it, but you're right." This type of person simply does not pay attention. He has eyes that don't see and ears that don't hear.

Another employee notices the problem but thinks to herself, "Well, so what?" Although she perceives things as they are, she fails to realize exactly what the problem is.

Next to her is an employee who not only notices the problem but understands that the problem must be eliminated. "This is terrible," he might say. "Something must be done about it."

Another employee goes on to think of concrete countermeasures to cope with the problem. "This is what should be done — why don't we do it like this?" However, she does not take action to implement a countermeasure.

Another employee is capable of taking the necessary action. He will notify the people in charge of the situation and put forward a resourceful proposal. Whenever possible, he will devise a proposal that he can himself implement within the scope of his responsibility. If it cannot be completed instantly, he will prepare a plan and start working on the things that *can* be done.

Most corporations hope for this last type of employee, the type who can bring a proposal to its realization. Unfortunately, few people have a natural tendency to react like this. The aim of the kaizen teian movement is to increase the number of resourceful workers. But it won't happen overnight. Kaizen teian is a continuous process in which success comes in small increments.

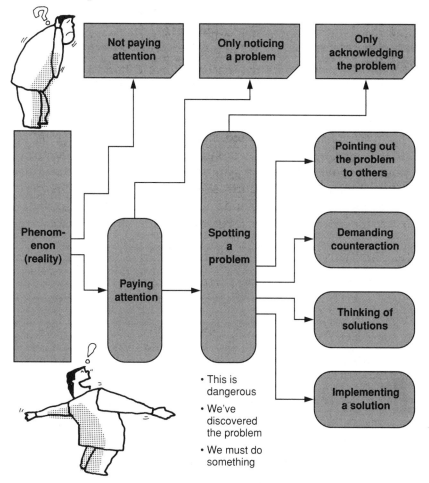

A PROCESS FOR CREATING COMPETENT EMPLOYEES

The first stage in preparing employees to do kaizen is to turn inattentive people into employees who can see that things aren't right. Ask them to look again at their workplace. Make sure they know the difference between normal and abnormal situations. This knowledge is essential to an understanding of the actual situation.

The second stage of kaizen proposal activities is to transform people who do notice things into people who can see the actual problems. They become aware of the standards and requirements of their jobs and they understand their jobs' objectives. In other words, the aim in stage 2 is to develop problem consciousness.

In stage 3, we work to convert people who know only that there is a problem somewhere into people who consider what should be done to fix it. These employees become active players in their jobs rather than mere spectators, as was the case before. They are true innovators, full of ideas, rather than employees who merely voice their discontent and complain about injustices.

In the fourth stage, we educate employees to implement their ideas. Unlike creative thought, implementation requires practical knowledge and special techniques. It also takes good judgment, powers of persuasion, and negotiating skills.

These skills and abilities are the hallmarks of an excellent employee. Kaizen activity offers a training ground for developing these abilities.

DISCUSSION QUESTIONS

What are two advantages to kaizen teian?

What are the disadvantages of effect-based proposal systems?

Why are bottom-up approaches to improvement better than top-down approaches?

11

Teian Is On-the-Job Training Through Three-Dimensional Evaluation

THE THREE OBJECTIVES OF KAIZEN ACTIVITY

Since the kaizen teian system develops the abilities of company employees, it is in fact a system for on-the-job training (OJT). In this respect it differs greatly from Western suggestion systems, which tend to be programs for awarding bonuses in exchange for better efficiency.

In a system based simply on the idea of an exchange of one thing for another, it is easy to create evaluation standards. All one has to do is to make a formula for calculating efficiency and then develop rules to provide bonus awards in proportion to the efficiency improvement. Once the effect of a suggestion has been measured, a chart determines the amount of the award automatically. (For that reason, Western suggestion systems make it difficult to determine the award amounts when the effect of a suggestion cannot be measured objectively.)

Things are not so simple in a kaizen teian (continuous improvement proposal) system, which is based on the concept of employee education. There is more to kaizen teian than simply determining the amount of the award; payment of a bonus represents only one part of the proposal activity.

The Japanese type of proposal system has in fact three main objectives:

1. *Participation:* Activating the organization by encouraging all employees to participate in kaizen teian activities.
2. *Development of abilities:* Developing abilities through kaizen activity. The aim is to acquire practical skills and the ability to realize ideas by learning to reassess a situation and to look at it from different angles.
3. *Effect:* The tangible and intangible effects that result from innovative solutions. This objective is conceived as a beneficial consequence of participation and development activities. It is not pursued as an end in itself. It is more important to encourage participation and promote development of the employees' skills and abilities; the effect will come as the result of these activities.

If we want to achieve all of these objectives, the kaizen teian system must do the following:

1. Facilitate communication between supervisors and frontline employees
2. Motivate frontline employees to do kaizen and encourage them to continue developing their skills
3. Train employees to reassess situations and consider various approaches to improvement

We cannot achieve all of these objectives by simply paying employees an award. In the kaizen teian system, awards have the following three meanings, each corresponding to a different objective:

- Appreciation for participation in kaizen activity
- Encouragement to further develop one's abilities
- Remuneration to communicate that the proposal was effective

Evaluation Standards Should Guide and Educate

How is proposal activity actually conducted? When a proposal system gives managers nothing but headaches, it is usually because the activities that are supposed to foster development of abilities, to educate, and to provide guidance have not been well integrated into the system. Instead, the focus is on "processing" the proposals (a bureaucratic term that no one likes), as if that were the most important part of the activity.

In an effort to change workers' perception that kaizen is something unpleasant, management studies other types of systems. It may try to imitate the proposal systems of other companies or even to copy their managerial and organizational structure. Little by little, however, it will forget the most important thing — the purpose of a kaizen proposal system.

Too often, evaluation standards and methods have become the pivotal component of the whole system. This type of system exhibits the following characteristics:

- The only thing communicated to the employees is the result of the evaluation.
- Evaluation standards are not published.
- Evaluation is done by someone other than a direct supervisor.

This is a system in which proposal evaluation is conducted behind closed doors. It seems to be based on the notion that people are better off when they don't know too much. Objectives such as education and skill development are virtually irrelevant in these proposal systems.

There are many management systems that are less extreme but still distinguish between education and guidance on one hand and evaluation on the other. Their evaluation standards often are created solely to determine the amount of the award; such proposal systems rarely provide opportunities for guidance and education.

Once proposal activity has become well established, it is driven by the know-how and experience of managers and leaders at the workplace; it also becomes a school of leadership. Any flaws in the system and its regulations are counterbalanced by the managers' enthusiasm in the workplace.

But until a proposal system becomes well established and each workplace accumulates sufficient experience with proposals and general know-how, confusion and perplexity are in store for everyone involved. The companies that succeed are those that persist in promoting proposal activities until the activities become firmly rooted in the corporate culture. Many companies get discouraged before this point, and so the activities proceed haphazardly and never really take off.

To prevent this from occurring, companies must document the experience and know-how gained at the workplace as manuals or standards that are accessible to everyone. Only then can these past experiences benefit other departments that are just starting out. Even companies where proposal activity is running smoothly and effectively can use this information to refine their methods of management.

A YARDSTICK THAT DIRECTS EMPLOYEES TOWARD GOOD KAIZEN PROPOSALS

In proposal systems that emphasize education and employee development, the people in charge of proposal activity are required not only to rate the proposals but also to write down helpful comments.

What kind of comments promote employee development? Comments such as "Please give it more thought" or "Try to find a more clever solution" are common. Although such statements are better than writing nothing at all, they don't really play a useful role. They make it clear that the reviewer was not happy with the proposal, but they provide no guidance, and thus nothing can be learned from them.

Think about it. If you want to be an innovator, you are always trying to find a more ingenious solution — that's why you're doing kaizen in the first place. People naturally want to think of clever solutions to earn bigger awards. But many would-be innovators don't understand what needs to be invented or how to find the clever solution. They need concrete advice on how to approach the problem, and suggestions about ideas that might have eluded them.

If you are a proposal reviewer, you may be thinking, "I would love to give concrete advice to everyone. But the fact is, I don't have any concrete advice to give." It may be that the best you can come up with is "Think of a more clever solution." Perhaps you were only recently put in charge of evaluating proposals for your workers and are just learning how to promote proposal activity. You want to provide as much solid advice as possible. But since you know little about training people, doing kaizen, or reviewing proposals, you worry that you have no advice to give.

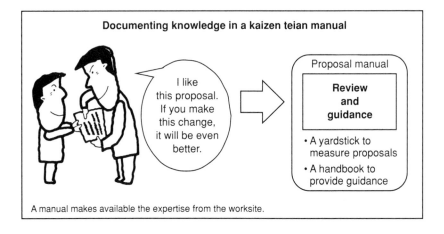

A manual makes available the expertise from the worksite.

People worry about kaizen proposals because they have an inadequate understanding of kaizen teian. To be sure, the concept is difficult to define in a few words. Most people can evaluate individual proposals generally as "good" or "not so good" but cannot explain why. It is even more difficult to explain how to improve a proposal.

That is why we need a "yardstick" for evaluating proposals. This yardstick should do the following:

1. It should provide an overall blueprint of the meaning of kaizen and the elements of a good proposal.

2. It should enable people to identify the position of each proposal in relation to the general blueprint.
3. It should show people at a glance the direction they need to look to improve their proposals.

A yardstick will also make the work of evaluating and advising much easier. In the past, standards for kaizen proposals were derived largely from values that were perceived differently by different people. Proposals were reviewed and guidance was provided primarily on the basis of the examiner's personal experience. A yardstick allows us to "standardize" personal experience.

Evaluation Standards that Address Different Levels

It is a good idea to create a comprehensive chart for evaluation standards. The *quick evaluation chart* shown on page 123 sorts proposals into three stages or levels (vertical axis):

Level 1: Observation and perception (pointing out problems and making them public)

Level 2: Original ideas (making proposals for improvement)

Level 3: Implemented proposals (proposals have been implemented and an effect has been achieved)

Grades of quality within each level are indicated with symbols (horizontal axis):

Δ = not bad, so-so
○ = good
◎ = very good

The quick evaluation chart has the following benefits:

• It makes it clear which essential conditions have been met by a particular proposal. It also clarifies what is expected from a proposal in the next higher level.

- It allows you to distinguish further whether a proposal on a given level is "not bad," "good," or "very good." This in turn helps the reviewer point out what would be required to raise the proposal to the next level, what kind of analysis or investigation is necessary, and what alternatives there are.

When using a quick evaluation chart, keep these points in mind:

1. The "effect" column applies only to the effects of proposals that have already been implemented. Do not use this column if the idea is not yet implemented, even if the proposal includes an "anticipated effect" or a "calculation of expected effect."
2. Simply grade each idea intuitively as so-so, good, or very good. Do not measure effect when the reward will be less than ¥1,000 ($7.00).
3. The economic effect of proposals that could be awarded more than ¥1,000 should be measured and evaluated.

The reasons for this are as follows:

- It is nonsense to evaluate the effect of an unimplemented idea by trying to calculate the estimated effect.
- An expected effect of several million yen from a proposal that has not been implemented has no value for evaluation purposes. On the other hand, an implemented proposal with an effect worth only a few thousand yen is very valuable. Ideas start having an effect only when they have been implemented.
- An award payment under ¥1,000 should be considered an investment in employee education. It should not be an award in exchange for the effect achieved. Therefore, there is no need for strict rules to calculate this effect. The evaluation should be based exclusively on the educational perspective; thus it can be made simply and intuitively.

Quick Evaluation Chart

Copyright © JHRA

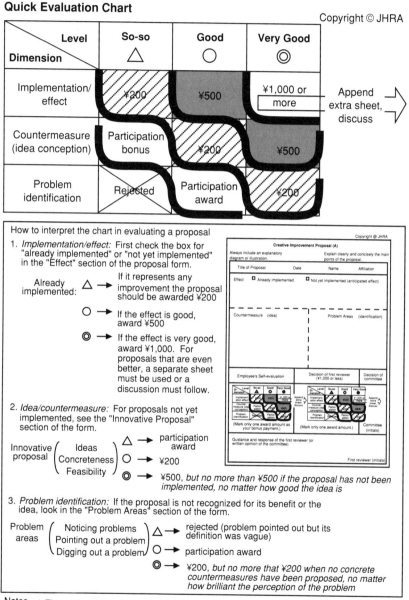

Level / Dimension	So-so △	Good ○	Very Good ◎
Implementation/ effect	¥200	¥500	¥1,000 or more
Countermeasure (idea conception)	Participation bonus	¥200	¥500
Problem identification	Rejected	Participation award	¥200

Append extra sheet, discuss →

How to interpret the chart in evaluating a proposal

1. *Implementation/effect:* First check the box for "already implemented" or "not yet implemented" in the "Effect" section of the proposal form.

Already implemented: △ → If it represents any improvement the proposal should be awarded ¥200

○ → If the effect is good, award ¥500

◎ → If the effect is very good, award ¥1,000. For proposals that are even better, a separate sheet must be used or a discussion must follow.

2. *Idea/countermeasure:* For proposals not yet implemented, see the "Innovative Proposal" section of the form.

Innovative proposal (Ideas, Concreteness, Feasibility)

△ → participation award

○ → ¥200

◎ → ¥500, *but no more than ¥500 if the proposal has not been implemented, no matter how good the idea is*

3. *Problem identification:* If the proposal is not recognized for its benefit or the idea, look in the "Problem Areas" section of the form.

Problem areas (Noticing problems, Pointing out a problem, Digging out a problem)

△ → rejected (problem pointed out but its definition was vague)

○ → participation award

◎ → ¥200, *but no more that ¥200 when no concrete countermeasures have been proposed, no matter how brilliant the perception of the problem*

Notes   1. The amount of the bonus and the level at which a bonus will be paid depends on the conditions at each company.

2. An immediate bonus should be paid for an implemented improvement and a dimension and level should be assigned to it.

- For most proposals that are awarded a bonus of only a few thousand yen, it is a waste of time and money to try to make fine distinctions and conduct precise calculations of the effect.*

A YARDSTICK FOR EVALUATING COUNTERMEASURES

Table A on page 125 shows a way to evaluate countermeasures to deal with problems. This is an adaptation of the quick evaluation chart that gives concrete meaning to the three stages at each of the three levels of quality.

Based on the definition of a problem as the difference between standard and actual circumstances, this chart is a tool for evaluating the methods that a proposal uses to resolve problems and the quality of its proposed countermeasures. Specifically, it measures the degree to which obstacles — defined by words with a negative meaning such as inconvenient, unpleasant, insufficient, defective, unsafe — are eliminated and assigns proposals to a certain level on the chart.

To give an example, when the "effect" stage receives a [double circle], this means that the situation has been fully corrected. Virtually all the negative words that used to describe it have been eliminated and the improved level has become the new standard. The chart shows the conditions that will be present when this level is achieved.

On the other hand, when the effect is assigned a Δ, this means that although most of the negative elements are still there, someone asked why things were like that — someone hit on an idea. Let's take a look at some typical patterns in proposals.

---

* See Japan Human Relations Association, ed., *Kaizen Teian 1: Developing Systems for Continuous Improvement Through Employee Suggestions* (Cambridge, Mass.: Productivity Press, 1992).

Table A:
Countermeasure Evaluation Chart
for "Negative" Problems

Level Quality	So-so △	Good ○	Very Good ◎
Effect of imple-mentation	Measure implemented immediately (Even if only temporary, still better than doing nothing.)	Measure deals with a cause of the problem (Some causes have not been addressed; problem only partially solved.)	Fundamental solution achieved (The most important causes largely have been eliminated.)
Idea development	Countermeasure discovered by accident; superficial remedy	Countermeasure deals with causes (Several important causes have been addressed.)	Countermeasure represents a fundamental solution (Deals with important causes of the problem.)
Percep-tiveness (problem identification)	Expression of discontent and deficiencies. Problem areas pointed out. (Obvious reasons pointed out.)	Main causes identified and pointed out.	Fundamental causes of the problem dug out, discovered, and pointed out.

Areas recommended for special attention: the ability to identify the real causes of problems, the ability to bring forth countermeasures dealing with real causes, the extent to which real causes are eliminated.

Perceptiveness △ + Idea Development △ = Effect △

At this level is the demand type of proposal. It simply expresses the fact that something is wrong, that a deficiency exists. In addition, it gives the most obvious reason for the problem, but this is only a superficial explanation.

On this level, we can expect only superficial countermeasures, ones dealing with symptoms rather than causes. Proposals developed under these circumstances are often rudimentary, since they were conceived incidentally, and with little planning. Although implementing them may be better than doing nothing at all, only limited and temporary effects will be achieved.

Bringing forth proposals at this level is still preferable to remaining at the "zero" level, where people don't care, feel no responsibility, and have no motivation. They never notice problems and so never point them out. By contrast, noticing problems and thinking of ways to correct them should be valued as positive. This is where kaizen activity starts. But if this is the best level we ever achieve, we will have problems.

Perceptiveness ○/◎ + Idea Development ○/◎ = Effect ○

We achieve this level when we identify the real causes of a problem. Since the countermeasures we propose deal with the real causes, several concrete problems can be eliminated.

However, we may have failed to see the most important aspect of the problem, our countermeasures may be less effective than they should be, or we may be unable to fully implement our proposal. Whatever the case, we still have not come up with a fundamental solution to our problem.

Of course, it is not always necessary to require fundamental solutions when kaizen activity is just beginning. The important thing at first is to keep making a lot of small but cumulative improvements. We must try to implement what we can, given existing limitations. If some benefit results, we should applaud such proposals and encourage people to come up with more.

However, we are still not satisfied at this level of performance. What we really want are fundamental solutions, solutions that are much more ingenious.

Perceptiveness ◎ + Idea Development ◎ = Effect ◎

At this level, the most important causes of problems have been correctly identified and a program of fundamental countermeasures has been put in place. Moreover, once these countermeasures are implemented, the problems are eliminated.

Even if the problem is minor, from an education and training viewpoint, the reviewer should acknowledge when an idea fulfills all the basic criteria: discovering the fundamental causes; proposing fundamental countermeasures; and implementing those countermeasures.

If the effect of the kaizen improvement is greater than what this category describes, rate the proposal in a higher category. Depending on the magnitude of the effect achieved, a higher evaluation and a higher bonus should be recommended.

Imperfect but Implementable Is Better than Ideal but Unimplementable

It is generally believed that the more widespread the problem, the more difficult it is to pursue its causes and propose countermeasures. Moreover, any proposals that are generated are more difficult to implement.

As employees gain experience, professional knowledge, and technical and negotiating skills, they should be encouraged to attack serious problems and produce a greater effect.

People who have been employed at a company for 10 years or more should automatically perform well in kaizen activity, producing far-reaching improvement ideas several times a year. Kaizen activity is useful for developing abilities and improving performance of employees at any level.

It is all right to aim at improvements that have a far-reaching effect; the problem with this approach is that it is effective only to the extent that such improvements can be implemented — otherwise it becomes counterproductive. What you have then are monumental suggestions that remain only dreams. While enthusiasm should be acknowledged and appreciated, corporations value concrete results. Painting a pretty picture of an effect that will be worth millions in savings is not appreciated. What is required is a real effect, even if it is worth only a little money.

That is why second-best countermeasures that can be implemented should be rated higher than ideal countermeasures that cannot be implemented. The approach you should cultivate in employees is to introduce improvements within a range where they can be implemented and then to develop kaizen abilities and skills that will permit people to expand their range of effectiveness.

Some people might object: "Isn't it true that some of the most brilliant ideas cannot be implemented only because of the situation and general prevailing conditions at a certain company? Shouldn't we sympathize with the employees who came up with such ideas?"

Sympathy is fine, but remember that what you are trying to develop in your employees is the ability to formulate kaizen proposals that can be implemented *despite* unfavorable conditions in the company. Anyone can come up with a brilliant proposal. It requires far better judgment and perceptiveness to formulate good ideas that can be implemented.

Some companies go so far as to accept only proposals that are already implemented. You might not want to go that far, but you should at least distinguish between ideas that are realistic and those that are not by awarding smaller bonuses to proposals that have not yet been implemented.

Even if a proposal has not been implemented, it can be awarded a small bonus. Such awards, which encourage further development and show appreciation for the employee's participation, should be regarded as sound investments in employee education.

A YARDSTICK FOR EVALUATING NEW OBJECTIVES AND TARGETS

A more comprehensive definition of *problem* includes the difference between the present situation and new standards or targets that we set for ourselves. In this case, a problem is "created" because the present conditions are not satisfactory in relation to this new ideal. Table B indicates levels of evaluation on the basis of this definition.

Table B:
Countermeasure Evaluation Chart
for "New Standard" Problems

Level / Dimension	So-so △	Good ○	Very Good ◎
Effect of implementation	Measure implemented immediately (Although it may be temporary, it does amount to a small improvement.)	Improvement to a new level (A higher level has been achieved.)	Higher level and higher targets have been achieved (Job objectives can now be accomplished much more effectively.)
Idea development	Method discovered accidentally	Concrete method is proposed (Method deals effectively with various job requirements.)	Proposed method has a dramatic effect (Method is very effective, achieving all important job targets.)
Perceptiveness (target setting)	Mere wishful thinking	A higher level has been established This means that the job will be • more pleasant, more comfortable • safer, undisturbed • faster, of better quality • more reliable, better organized	A dramatically different target has been set This can be applied to one of the following: • What is the purpose of the job? • Can sales volume be multiplied? • Can costs be reduced? • Can this process be eliminated?

Areas recommended for special attention: the extent to which real objectives were achieved; the extent to which the measures help achieve these objectives; and how efficiently these objectives are achieved.

We can also use the word *task* here instead of *problem,* which has a passive connotation; this is aggressive kaizen. Problems in this sense are really tasks that we take on to reach a higher standard. Let us take a closer look at yardsticks for measuring this kind of kaizen.

Perceptiveness Δ = Idea Development

This rating means that what the proposal describes amounts to little more than wishful thinking. This kind of proposal might relate to a new line of business or a new product. It might say something like, "If we only had a machine like this," or "If we only could do it that way" — an "if only" proposal.

In fact, the proposal might be a brilliant idea. Even the examiner will describe it in superlatives. If it could be implemented, superlatives would certainly be in order.

But the problem is that there are no concrete means that would make it possible to implement such a proposal. Unfortunately, it cannot be brought to that final stage. To put it bluntly, even a child could come up with a proposal like this.

What is expected from adult innovators is a concrete method or idea that can be implemented. This does not mean we should tell people not to dream. On the contrary, we should encourage them to develop their own abilities and skills so they can *realize* their dreams.

Nothing new will come from a serene environment where everyone is happy with the way things are. Neither will it come from an environment where the best that people can do is to complain about deficiencies and indulge in wishful thinking.

The more you wish for your dream to come true and the higher your aspirations and objectives, the more likely you are to reach a stage when you will begin thinking "I have to implement some of these!" At that point your ideas will become more realistic.

Perceptiveness ○ + Idea Development ○ = Effect △/○

From wishful thinking, it is not too far to the next stage, when people desire to change something — whether it be to make the job more pleasant or to do something faster. The next step usually involves more concrete thinking, expressed in terms such as "How should I improve this situation?" and "I wonder if this problem could be solved like this."

Once this stage has been reached, the methods used become more concrete and realistic. They may not be highly creative, but at least they are capable of being implemented. Moreover, the effect may be minimal, but if a modest degree of improvement is achieved and accumulated over time, then the improvement is valuable.

Perceptiveness ◎ + Idea Development ◎ = Effect ○/◎

At this level, we aspire to even higher standards. Our target is an idea of how things should be in the future, as opposed to simple kaizen based on the present situation. Our improvement proposals are pulled from our thinking about how to reach this target.

With luck, we should be able to find the most effective and productive method of achieving this target. At this stage, we are evaluated not only on the standard that we aim for, but also on how effectively we achieve it.

Two Approaches to Kaizen

Tables A and B highlight the two basic approaches to kaizen and problem solving. The approach outlined in Table A is to determine the principle causes of a negative element we perceive ("inconvenience" or "danger," for example), then choose a method that eliminates these causes one by one. This method, called the *push method*, usually involves a number of improvements that have a cumulative effect.

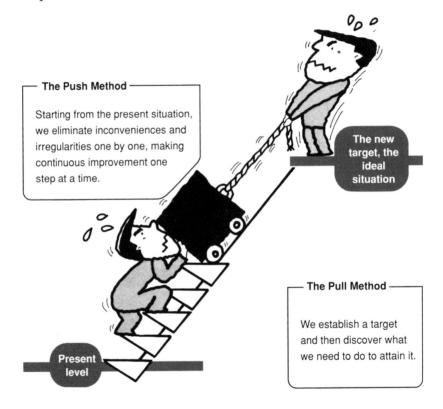

The method outlined in Table B consists of first setting a higher level or target and then coming up with concepts for achieving it. You can also start by asking, "What is the purpose of this job?" and then determine the best method to realize the job objectives. This method, called the *pull method*, can lead to fundamentally different yet qualitatively better improvements.

The method that analyzes and eliminates the negative elements is a solid and reliable approach. Sometimes, however, it leads us down a dead-end street. In such situations, try using a different yardstick, which is described in the next section.

A COMMON YARDSTICK FOR PROPOSAL WRITERS AND REVIEWERS

The quick evaluation chart is a tool for determining the amount of bonus awards as well as a yardstick for guiding employee development through kaizen. That is why we distinguish between the present and the next level of the kaizen process. An evaluation system that focuses only on the results of a proposal will have no educational value and will fail to provide guidance.

But when managers work alongside frontline employees in studying the improvement process, they become more able to explain why a better grade should be given to a better proposal. When an employee submits many proposals over time, the level of those proposals will rise. During this process, employees will come to view kaizen as a yardstick with which they can measure their environment. In this way, employees will grow as innovators and will further develop their kaizen skills and abilities.

It is said that good results come from a good process, and this applies as well to education and guidance for improvement activities. Only by examining the improvement process will we achieve good results. What we really want, however, is for employees themselves to understand the kaizen process and to evaluate their own ideas. Self-teaching is the best way to develop skills. Employees should not need a manager's guidance to improve their level of kaizen.

When we use kaizen as a yardstick, we can more or less determine where our proposal would fall within the system and what its deficiencies are. Not only that, we can also see what to improve next, and how to formulate better proposals.

Those who provide guidance will also benefit from knowing precisely where a certain proposal fits in, which areas should receive praise, and which areas need more work. Too often, reviewers make banal statements that offer employees no guidance on how to improve their proposals. Without meaningful feedback, employees may lose their motivation to write proposals; they may even become alienated from the kaizen proposal system.

Conversely, it's not good to reject a proposal by saying, "It's not a fundamental improvement and therefore is not good enough." Such a comment would be perceived as needlessly picky.

There is always some positive way to evaluate a proposal. By showing reviewers how to position a proposal, the kaizen yardstick helps us to do this. In the final analysis, kaizen measures how well managers are able to lead those employees who work under them.

Raising an Idea from Seed to Fruition

To understand the concept of a kaizen yardstick, let's look at the growth of a plant. In the beginning, the plant is only a seed. This seed corresponds to the discovery of our problem, or task. Just as nothing will grow where there are no seeds, where there are no problems — or when we fail to notice problems — no proposals of any kind can come up; it seems that there is no need for any. Discovering the problem, then, is the first step toward kaizen activity.

The "bud" emerges at the next stage, when we are ready to solve the problem. No matter how many problems we notice, unless we are ready to solve them, we are stuck at the first level. Only when we are moved to ask, "Couldn't we do something about this?" do we take a step toward solving our problem.

Evaluation Depends on the Kind of Yardstick You Use

Smart employees are those who discover problems among the complaints of customers or other workers and use that knowledge for further education and improvement.

The next step is to generate ideas and formulate creative proposals. This can be likened to caring for a bud so that it produces a stem and leaves. Although ideas come in varying degrees of quality, each does something to improve the situation.

Just as flowers sometimes bloom without giving fruit, so do kaizen proposals sometimes fail to produce the expected effect,

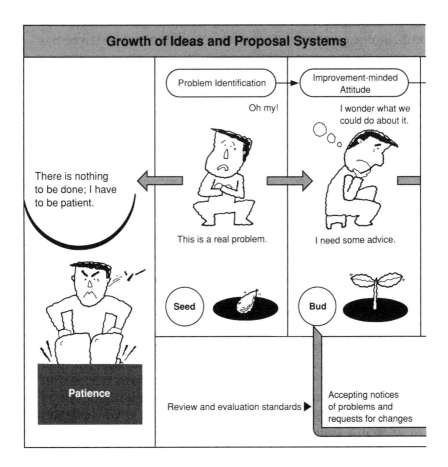

even if they have been implemented. On the other hand, without the flower (implementation of a proposal), there is no chance that the plant will bear fruit (effect of a proposal).

Like plants, ideas start from seeds. Some ideas will wither before reaching fruition, but some will produce beautiful flowers as well as the fruits we were growing them for.

The differences between various proposal systems rest in the stage of growth at which ideas are recognized and evaluated. Some companies evaluate ideas only at the stage when they are bearing fruit; others recognize ideas at the "budding" stage.

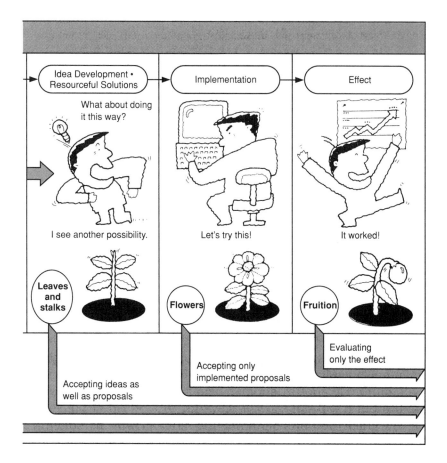

Some companies think that the "seed" stage is significant and should be recognized. Others think that the employee's attitude toward kaizen and approach to the process itself should be evaluated.

If our strategy is to develop kaizen activity by caring for and cultivating ideas, we must use a three-dimensional standard for evaluation. This standard covers the whole range, from seed to fruition, from accurate perception of the problem to presentation of a resourceful idea to the final effect.

DISCUSSION QUESTIONS

What are the three objectives of a kaizen teian system?

In what ways can an evaluation system promote those objectives?

What three general categories of proposals are recognized in a quick evaluation chart?

What does it mean to say that kaizen teian activity should be evaluated according to a three-dimensional standard?

12

Teian Is a Barometer
of Leadership

GUIDANCE THAT ENGENDERS IDEAS AND CULTIVATES CREATIVE THINKING

An essential element of kaizen teian activity is the guidance that managers provide to workers. Proposal systems based on implemented improvements are really a kind of on-the-job training. They give frontline employees regular opportunities to make constructive proposals as well as to receive a practical education.

Many companies today recognize the importance of this aspect of kaizen teian activity. The proposal rules of a growing number of companies state expressly that the role of management is to provide guidance regarding kaizen proposals. Many companies conduct sessions during which managers and supervisors study kaizen proposals.

How to Kill Creative Thinking and How to Cultivate It

To some people, providing constructive guidance does not come naturally. Unless it is clear what kind of guidance is needed and how it should be provided, help can be counterproductive.

The tendency to provide counterproductive help is often seen in newly appointed leaders, administrators, and reviewers. Inexperienced managers often take an over-serious approach to providing guidance. Their rigid and uncompromising attitudes often lead to misunderstandings. Proposal review sessions are apt to turn into nitpicking arguments, in which the proposal writer is treated as either a criminal or a student trying to pass entrance exams.

Guidance should not be confused with criticism. Finding fault with proposals and pointing out their weaknesses can become addictive. Such an attitude is not effective for educating proposal writers about kaizen teian. This negative guidance kills creative thinking.

To a manager, an employee's proposal may appear to be rife with shortcomings. With factors such as cost, safety, the effect on downstream processes, and difficulty of implementation to consider, managers could find reasons to obliterate just about any proposal.

Unfortunately, some managers reject employees' proposals because they feel threatened by their ideas. Such attitudes are not useful. Employees who have become managers tend to have better experience, knowledge, and judgment than those who work for them. Instead of using their expertise to criticize the shortcomings of proposals, they should be using it in a positive way to inspire creative thinking and to improve the quality of the employee's proposal.

For example, even in a poor proposal, they must focus on its strong points and thus nourish the writer's motivation. Rather than merely pointing out defects, they should explain how proposals can be improved, give hints for how to go about it, and point the proposal writer toward a better solution. Effective managers learn to share their own experience and knowledge to reinforce others' ideas. It is their job to cultivate creative thinking, not to kill it.

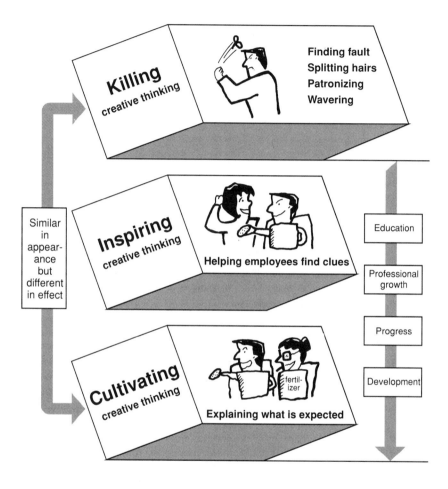

The critical reviewer will crush the ideas of innovators and in the end destroy their motivation and desire to point out problems. What this type of manager does is like stepping on fragile flowers. By contrast, the constructive reviewer will bring new life into kaizen activity. By recognizing the value of a proposal and working to reinforce its positive aspects, this type of manager can provide training for more demanding improvements.

Patronizing, Indecision, and the Pen Pal Game

One way to kill creative thinking is to take an irresponsible, patronizing approach. Reading in the company's kaizen teian procedure manual that they should thank employees for their proposals, some managers take the instruction literally, without realizing its full meaning.

When these managers write comments on an employee's proposal form, they say something like, "Thank you very much for your proposal. It is a wonderful idea." Sometimes they respond to employee inquiries with a flurry of say-nothing notes, as if they were writing to a pen pal about the weather.

Despite the nice words, however, the proposal remains unimplemented. The problem is that these managers cannot explain what to do to make a proposal work better and cannot make decisions about implementation.

When on top of that they add a note saying, "Please don't hesitate to write another proposal in the future," it sounds like a bad joke. Maybe they can get away with this once or twice, but the employees will not forgive them forever. Soon everyone thinks that no matter what kind of a proposal they make, the supervisor will never do anything about it, so why bother. They will decide that no one will make them look like fools again, and proposals will dry up for good.

The supervisor and the administrator are really the ones under scrutiny when a proposal is submitted; first-line employees understand this perfectly. As soon as an employee submits a proposal, he or she begins sizing up the supervisor's attitude toward the proposal and toward the particular job, gauging whether the supervisor has good judgment.

If employees feel that their proposals are not accepted because their manager is narrow-minded, they will feel cheated. Employees are extremely sensitive to the reactions of their supervisors; they can detect when a manager just wants to avoid an issue or accepts a proposal only pro forma to stop it in its tracks.

Review and Evaluation Should Be Based on the Standards Set for the Job

Although it is wrong to focus on an proposal's weak points, it is equally wrong to provide overindulgent guidance and evaluation that does not identify defects. Neither approach has educational value, and neither explains to the innovator what kind of proposal would be preferable. The net result is that the proposal writer's confidence is undermined. The problem with both approaches is that the objectives and targets of a given job have not been made the main criteria for evaluation and guidance.

What Is Guidance?

The Japanese word for *guidance* can be written with characters that mean "cooperation of kindred spirits," "showing the way," and "activating." When people who work in the same place are of the same mind, they will usually be willing to show each other the right way, to take the initiative to launch a new project.

The first step in this direction must be what we call a guidance of minds — clarifying the objectives and targets for the workers in the workplace. This will also serve as a basis for proposal evaluation standards. The absence of such an objective basis leads to evaluations that are based on the reviewer's own preferences and subjective interpretations, which are sometimes too harsh or too indulgent.

Kaizen means destroying present conditions, no matter how small the scale of destruction. Most of the time, the proposals and ideas submitted have no precedents, which makes a response difficult. Even when we have examples of how evaluation should be done and of how to apply proposals, sooner or later we will have to deal with proposals that are outside our scope of reference.

That is why it is necessary to have a basic method for interpreting proposals. Such a method must be based on the objectives and targets of a given workplace. This is the only ground for standards that can be shared by managers and workers. Both sides will find it understandable and persuasive.

Standards simplify the evaluation process. The fact is that different people have different value systems. When people try to judge a proposal using their own value systems, communication between them may become very complicated. At the very least, decisions about job improvements should be shared by all the employees in the workplace. This is possible only when professional objectives and targets are used as a standard and common ground.

When it is unclear precisely what those objectives are, that usually means the managers are unaware of how to identify those objectives. That being the case, the training of managers and administrators in a kaizen teian system should include, aside from proposal regulations and review standards, a basic explanation of the real objectives and targets of each department.

But, you say, that kind of professional training is *always* required of people who make decisions. That is just the point. There is no special field to study, no special training required for kaizen teian. Kaizen teian is nothing special. It is simply changing the way we do our job. That's all there is to it.

This training should be given not only to administrators and managers, but also to proposal writers. You cannot learn how to write proposals in a vacuum. In fact, learning about kaizen is nothing more than learning how to do the job.

Proposals as a Barometer of Leadership Ability

What managers most dislike about kaizen activity is that its initial stages reveal the problems of their own department.

Because kaizen begins with the identification of existing problems, it presumes acknowledgement of one's own prior willingness to tolerate those problems. People must admit, in essence, that they have been doing a poor job. Recognition of that fact is painful enough that it is tempting to sweep a revealing proposal under the carpet.

In addition, if a large number of proposals are submitted, people assume that the workplace is in serious trouble. This is not necessarily the case. A large number of proposals may mean that people are finally facing up to problems and suggesting something be done about them. It means that people have the will and the skills to solve their problems. Indeed, the number of proposals submitted serves as a barometer to leadership ability in the manager.

Effective Proposals Are the Responsibility of Managers

It is sometimes said that proposals are made only in departments that have skillful reviewers. The fact is that nothing will come of any idea, no matter how brilliant it may be, unless it is approved by the person who first evaluates it.

It is easy to crush proposals — to leave so little breathing room that new ideas suffocate. On the other hand, even a modest proposal can flourish if it gains the notice and approval of a supervisor.

To take the attitude that employees are to blame for subpar proposals is irresponsible and counterproductive. After all, kaizen proposals put no great demands on employees; we are not talking about breakthrough inventions and epoch-making ideas. We are talking about ideas that any employee could come up with. The problem is not the limited abilities of employees. The problem is that no one is motivated to come forward with problems that everyone knows about. The blame for that problem rests squarely on management's shoulders.

THREE LINES TO AVOID

The following lines should never be used when providing guidance regarding kaizen proposals:

1. That is so ordinary.
2. We have no precedent for that approach.
3. Other companies don't do it that way.

Most proposal writers have heard such lines before. Reviewers and supervisors usually resort to them when they can't think of anything else to say.

Kaizen Is Doing Normal Things Normally

The judgment that an idea is "ordinary" often delivers the deathblow to that idea. Clearly, *all* kaizen ideas can be seen as ordinary. Kaizen is not a special gift; its very essence is seeking ordinary solutions for ordinary problems. It is only natural for a production department to be committed to high-quality goods. But unless the department is extremely resourceful, it may produce shoddy goods anyway.

Likewise, it is only natural for the service department to treat customers with courtesy. But since customer service representatives are only human, service can slip without continual efforts to improve it.

The submission of "ordinary" proposals indicates something important about a workplace. It means that in that particular workplace it has not been possible to do business in an ordinary way. If such proposals are rejected because they are ordinary, people ultimately will stop submitting commonsense improvement ideas.

Granted, most proposal reviewers would love to get their hands on proposals that would have an earth-shaking effect. But the company clearly has a problem if it expects such ideas to come from first-line employees. This kind of proposal should be expected primarily from the managers and specialists charged with making important decisions.

If anyone in the company could come up with break-through innovations like this, there would be no reason for hiring experts at high salaries. At the same companies where simple ideas from the frontline employees are rejected as too ordinary, those who draw substantial salaries are probably chasing trivial improvements, and everyone probably has their hands full processing customer complaints. No wonder there is no time for really valuable innovations and major reforms.

For that reason, demanding big-ticket ideas from first-line employees is a clear portent of disaster. It indicates that the company has forgotten elementary business rules for controlling costs and lost sight of basic rules of production.

What is the situation like at companies where common employees can implement ordinary, commonsense proposals? Needless to say, things are organized so that specialists and managers are left free to concentrate on higher-level innovations and on substantial reforms.

You Never Know Until You Try

In some companies, proposals are rejected merely because there is no precedent for a given proposal or because "they don't do it that way" at other companies. Companies that operate this way might as well abolish their proposal systems and give up. No proposal, however small, has a precedent, because it represents a new way of doing things. If managers accepted only those proposals that had precedents, no progress would be made at all.

Every job has two sides to it. One is the operation itself which is done according to a set of rules. The other component, however, is the operator, who has the discretion to alter existing conditions by revising methods and aiming for higher standards. Kaizen is effective only when we have the courage to break up existing conditions by introducing "unprecedented" innovations that defy the present order of things.

As for the claim that other companies aren't doing it this way, this is no argument against a proposal. On the contrary, doing something differently might be the thing that distinguishes your company from other companies and thus gives it a competitive edge. If your goal is merely to imitate what other companies are doing, then you don't need to solicit proposals from your own employees.

Of course, it is understandable that people hesitate to take risks. Every employee wants to protect his or her position by playing it safe. Doing something in a new way leaves you open to failure and may incur extra expenses.

Remember, however, proposals that motivate will not destroy existing conditions all at once. Rather, change comes gradually, in small steps whose effects accumulate as small improvements are continually implemented. If one thing doesn't work, we try something else. Employees must become accustomed to the process of trial and error, at least temporarily.

It is also important to make sure everyone knows what kind of bonus to expect for a proposal. If some bonuses are paid for proposals that don't amount to much, it is not money wasted. If we can motivate first-line employees by paying them a bonus, we have made a good and inexpensive investment. It is also a good investment in employee education to award a large bonus for an extraordinary proposal.

In sum, it is better to turn a blind eye to the small imperfections of some proposals than to crush an idea early by holding it up to rigid evaluation standards. Flexibility is the key. If you want to see more innovators coming forward, you need to handle proposals in an optimistic manner. Be enthusiastic. Let people experiment. You never know what will work until you try it.

DISCUSSION QUESTIONS

What role do managers play in promoting kaizen teian?

Specifically, what things should a manager do to provide constructive feedback during proposal evaluation?

Why should proposals never be rejected on the grounds that they are too ordinary or too different?

Why is it important to award bonuses for even small improvements?

PART FOUR

Kaizen Teian Examples

The value of kaizen activity grows as managers and employees work together in the workplace. To better understand the human interaction and the mutual exchange of information involved in kaizen, let's take a look at the specific experiences of proposal writers in five different businesses.

The Japan Human Relations Association holds annual public meetings in three areas of Japan to address these issues. This chapter introduces examples of experiences discussed at these meetings, as well as other examples recommended to us by various companies and published in our magazine *Ingenuity and Invention*. The companies described in the examples are

- Hakutsuru Shuzō (White Crane Sake Brewing Co.)
- TDK, Ltd.
- Mikkabi-chō Agricultural Cooperative
- Sony Kōda, Ltd.
- Toyota Motor Co.

Kaizen that Saves Work and Energy

(Hakutsuru Shuzo)
[White Crane Sake Brewing Co.]
by Kōhei Ueda

The region of Japan called Nada Gogō is well known for its sake breweries. Hakutsuru Shuzo, founded 240 years ago, is a sake manufacturer with a long tradition in that area.

I work at the manufacturing plant's headquarters. We produce and sell various types of sake, from clear White Crane sake brands to plum wines, brandies, and the sweet sake that is used as seasoning. We also import and sell wines and other products. We use aluminum cans that can hold from 35 milliliters to 18 liters, paper containers, and various glass containers and bottles.

I am in charge of several lines of these products. One of the operations that I supervise is a filling line for 1.8-liter bottles.

IMPROVING SAFETY IN THE BOTTLING PLANT

Two years ago, I began participating in our kaizen proposal system. The first problem I worked on involved doors in the plant that were often opened forcefully without warning. There were accidents from time to time when employees got slammed behind the opening door. When the employees were holding bottles, serious injuries sometimes occurred, and it was a mess to clean up.

The countermeasure we devised was to paint a line on the floor marking the path of the outer edge of the door. No one was supposed to stand within or place anything inside the area marked by that line.

Another problem we worked on was injuries that employees sustained while making frequent adjustments under the conveyor belt of the production line. People routinely bumped their heads and their rear ends trying to stand up too soon.

We did a couple of things to resolve this. One was to paint lines on the floor next to the conveyor, with footprints to indicate where the feet had to be in order to stand up without bumping anything.

We also discovered that the long visor on the work caps kept people from seeing the line and the footprints. Our solution was to shorten the visor, which widened the employees' field of view.

When I first began writing suggestions years ago, I was greatly disappointed by the feedback I got. The manager who reviewed them told me that my ideas were little more than com-

plaints and didn't rise to the level of "kaizen." He suggested that I work on ideas related to the safety of the machines or measures to reduce costs. When I looked at the operations that I was responsible for, I noticed a number of mechanical problems and other deficiencies.

One proposal we implemented involved a filling machine. The machine was washed with very hot water, and this made its cylinders and rings expand and obstruct the movement of its pistons. When the pistons get stuck, the employee operating the machine has to use a tool to pry them up. This was a dangerous operation since the machine was still moving, and it was also hard on the joints of the machine.

We asked ourselves why the washing had to be so troublesome. Since the problem was caused by the expansion of the parts, we decided to fix it by constructing a cooling device.

We used a plastic pipe and scrap material to put together a cold-water shower system to cool down the machine after washing. With this device in place, the pistons moved freely 100 percent of the time instead of 50 percent. Also, the washing is now much more effective, which considerably extends the life span of the machine parts. Most important, the device meant that employees no longer had to perform a dangerous operation.

I am fortunate to work with good friends whose help with kaizen proposals is always invaluable. Our group of six people is like a family.

The method we use in our group is to get together and try to answer the question, "What's wrong with this?" Each of us can ask questions or answer them. Our basic proposal activity is to ask questions until we arrive at the cause of the problem, then come up with countermeasures.

One problem we addressed this way involved measures to prevent carton jamming in a feeding device. Our carton is pretty sturdy, so why did it keep jamming the machine? Instead of one carton, it takes up two cartons at a time. "Maybe the pressure on it is too strong." "Do you think the counterweight might be too heavy?" "Let's experiment." We tried varying the size of the counterweight that keeps the pressure on the stack of cartons. Ultimately, we settled on one kilogram as the weight that created the optimum pressure so that the machine took up only one carton at a time.

Another employee, Chosan, tired of getting hot water and broken glass down his boots, came up with the idea to close the top of the boots. The invention — "Chosan's improved tall boots with closed top" — was made with rubber shower caps that were cut to fit the top of each boot.

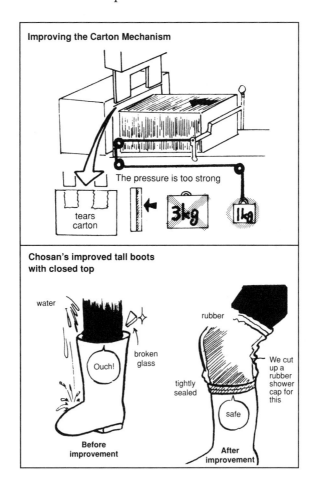

One of my tasks involves measuring the temperature of the sake on my line. I used to do this by holding the thermometer with my hand. This tied up my hands, and if an incident on the line needed my attention, I would have to begin the measurement all over after fixing the problem.

An idea came to me one day as I watched gymnastics on television. I was impressed by the way the gymnast gripped the parallel bars by wrapping her knees around them. Maybe we could wrap something around the thermometer to hold it in place, I thought. After some experimentation, we created a rubber stopper to hold the thermometer in the mouth of the bottle. Now we don't have to spend all that time holding the thermometer, and we have had no more accidents.

One of the big hits among our kaizen proposals was a device for turning on the hot water shower only when it was required. This shower washes the surface of the bottles; the water temperature ranges from 40 to 50 degrees centigrade. When the bottles are not coming out, the hot water goes down the drain.

Working together, we made a device that turned the shower on when the bottles were under the opening, and off after 10 seconds, when they had moved beyond the shower. This produced the equivalent of about $4,000 in annual savings on each line. We were able to apply this proposal to a number of other lines besides our own.

Big hit number two came up when we went on to ask why we had to use a hot water shower in the first place, since it costs money to heat it. When we raised the question, we got all kinds of "good reasons" from the senior employees:

"Cold water won't get the dirt off the bottles."

"Sake sticks to the bottle like glue."

"If you abruptly cool the hot sake, it will spoil."

"We can't use cold water because I would catch cold from it."

"If we use cold water, the bottles will break."

"We've been using hot water for 20 years — that's the end of it!"

Despite this resistance, we got them to let us conduct an experiment. (We got a little wet in the process and understood some of the veteran workers' complaints!) A sampling test that compared the extent of cleaning and the percentage of broken bottles using cold and hot water showed no substantial difference in these results.

The day the results of the experiment were announced, we stopped using hot water for our line. The financial effect of this change was a cost savings equivalent to more than $40,000 a year. But most important, the work was now easier and more pleasant. Without our proposal system, it would have been impossible to change the old way of doing things and implement a new method, because no one dared to challenge an old tradition.

Kaizen Proposal Activity for Improved Manufacturing Maintenance

(TDK, Ltd.)
by Shigeki Yamazaki

I work in the TDK plant in Shizuoka, Japan (near Mt. Fuji), which produces magnets used in engines of cars and other vehicles. We also produce magnets in Chiba prefecture, as well as overseas in Mexico and Taiwan. I am in charge of maintenance and repair for the machines on the manufacturing line.

Our company's kaizen teian activities have taken firm root, building gradually over time. In 1986, the company placed third among Japanese companies in the number of proposals per person.

With this kind of momentum and with continued resourcefulness, we don't have to go out of our way to promote proposal activity.

When I first started making proposals, I was trying to fulfill the quota that had been set for us. Once I started writing, though, I was surprised at how many other things occurred to me. Ideas about other potentially interesting proposals easily came to mind, and the number of proposals I submitted grew steadily.

My company gave bookstore certificates as awards for unimplemented proposals or elementary-level implemented proposals. These were a wonderful incentive to me to continue developing improvement ideas.

The following year, my perception of what proposals should be about changed. I understood that I had to develop and use my know-how to make the best use of our equipment.

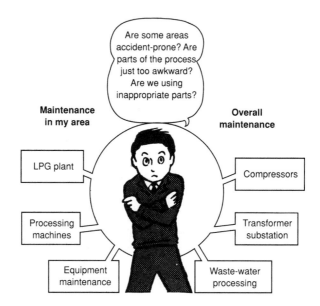

Resourceful improvements are a necessity in my work. Especially when receiving new equipment, I used caution and stayed aware of the possibility that some parts might have defects. Since I knew the problem areas, the number of proposals I submitted kept growing.

CONSULTATIONS WITH PEOPLE IN PRODUCTION

The important thing for me was to know what method the people in production really used. Even if we have good ideas, they are meaningless unless people are willing to act on them. During consultations with production workers, I got a better understanding of the problems they faced. My own proposal activity definitely took off because of these consultations.

Some people praised our kaizen proposals, finding machines safer and easier to use. Others were not completely satisfied and thought things should be further improved or done another way. I learned that even if you think you've got the answer, you need to listen carefully to what other people have to say.

Sometimes it was hard to write proposals. There were all kinds of obstacles, like feeling too tired, or realizing your solution is not good enough. I was aiming for a quota, however, so I wrote my name and the type of proposal on the proposal forms ahead of time for the number I had targeted. I also kept a diary in which I would write notes relating to proposals and relevant ideas for future reference.

PRACTICAL KAIZEN: IMPROVING A CONVEYOR SYSTEM

A series of presses stamped parts as a preliminary process. The stamped parts were placed on trays and the trays were moved along an auxiliary line onto a main line conveyor for further processing. Sometimes the trays coming onto the main line conveyor would collide with other trays already on the conveyor. This created a jam that stopped the line.

The improvement we devised was to install a photoelectric eye at each intersection, connected to a switch on each auxiliary line conveyor. This setup detects when a tray is passing by, and at which point it prevents the auxiliary line from moving new trays onto the main line. This effectively solved the problem.

PRACTICAL KAIZEN: IMPROVING A SUCTION-PICKUP DEVICE

Another improvement involved a vacuum pickup device for removing molded products and transporting them to the

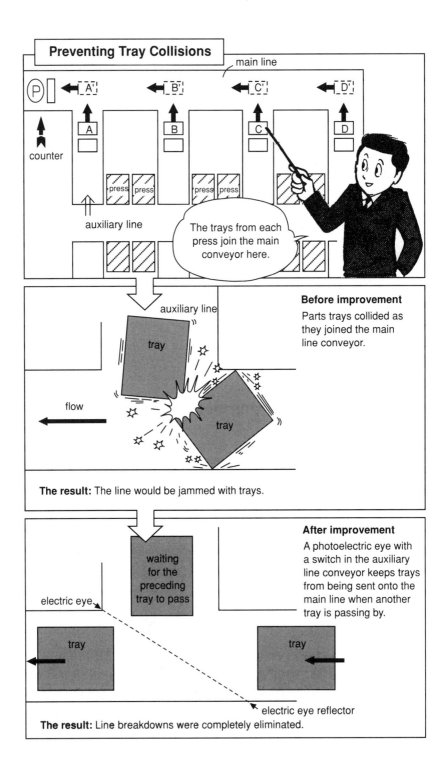

next process. This device was equipped with a detection device that was supposed to sound a warning when it did not feel the suction cup pick up the part.

The problem was that the detector "lied," indicating that parts were left behind when they were not, or that parts were picked up when in fact some were left behind. This frustrated the operators to no end, since they never knew the real situation and were always checking false alarms or trying to continue the process with pieces still in the machine.

Working together, our team devised a new system that used a photoelectric switch to detect when the pieces were picked up. This new detector was connected to a display panel with one light for the position of each piece on the tray. As each piece was picked up, the light for its position went on, providing a simple and mistake-proof way for the operator to check the pickup.

PRACTICAL KAIZEN: A BETTER WAY TO CLEAN
THE VACUUM SYSTEM

Our plant uses a lot of suction cup pickup devices to remove the parts from the processing machinery. Unfortunately, these pickups sucked up a lot of dust and debris in addition to the parts. This diminished the suction and led to errors in the pickup detection equipment.

To clean the generator and the pipes, an operator would block off the main air flow below each suction cup. This forced the air to blow out through the suction opening, and the dust and debris along with it. This method of cleaning was very inefficient, however, since operators had to clean each suction cup individually.

Our solution was to connect all the suction cups to the same system. The air flow was electronically reversed and all the cups could be cleaned simultaneously at regularly scheduled times. This was a much more efficient way to handle the cleaning.

Mistake-proofing a Parts-pickup Device

The operator knew when product was left behind because a buzzer would sound.

vacuum pickup device

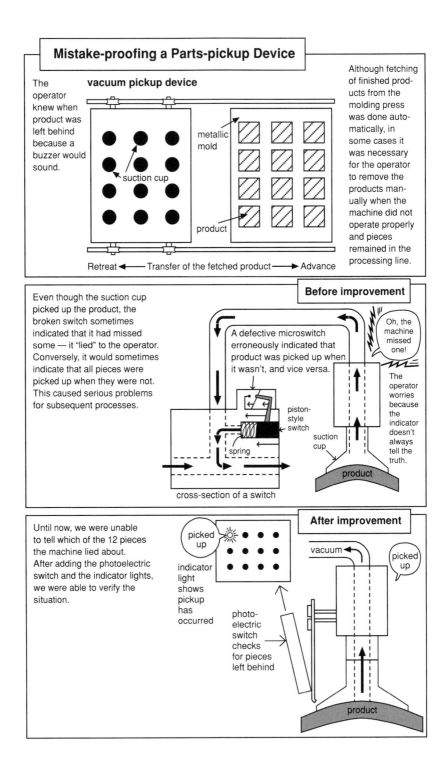

metallic mold

suction cup

product

Retreat ◄——— Transfer of the fetched product ———► Advance

Although fetching of finished products from the molding press was done automatically, in some cases it was necessary for the operator to remove the products manually when the machine did not operate properly and pieces remained in the processing line.

Before improvement

Even though the suction cup picked up the product, the broken switch sometimes indicated that it had missed some — it "lied" to the operator. Conversely, it would sometimes indicate that all pieces were picked up when they were not. This caused serious problems for subsequent processes.

A defective microswitch erroneously indicated that product was picked up when it wasn't, and vice versa.

Oh, the machine missed one!

The operator worries because the indicator doesn't always tell the truth.

piston-style switch

spring

suction cup

product

cross-section of a switch

After improvement

Until now, we were unable to tell which of the 12 pieces the machine lied about. After adding the photoelectric switch and the indicator lights, we were able to verify the situation.

picked up

indicator light shows pickup has occurred

vacuum ◄——

picked up

photo-electric switch checks for pieces left behind

product

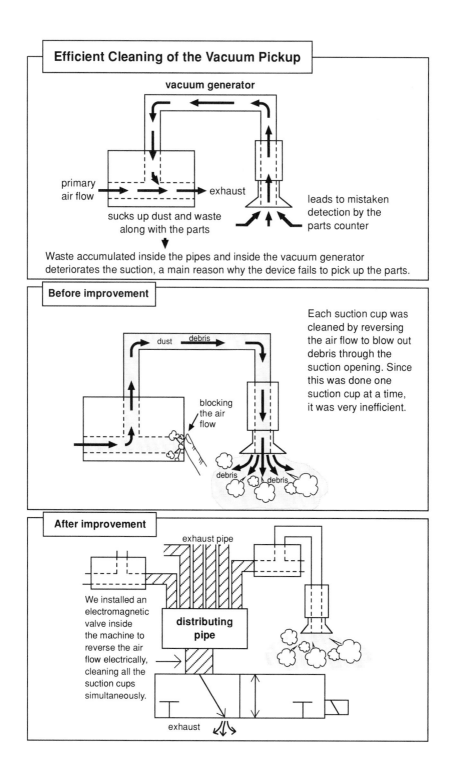

Efficient Cleaning of the Vacuum Pickup

vacuum generator

primary air flow → exhaust

sucks up dust and waste along with the parts

leads to mistaken detection by the parts counter

Waste accumulated inside the pipes and inside the vacuum generator deteriorates the suction, a main reason why the device fails to pick up the parts.

Before improvement

dust   debris

blocking the air flow

debris   debris

Each suction cup was cleaned by reversing the air flow to blow out debris through the suction opening. Since this was done one suction cup at a time, it was very inefficient.

After improvement

exhaust pipe

We installed an electromagnetic valve inside the machine to reverse the air flow electrically, cleaning all the suction cups simultaneously.

distributing pipe

exhaust

The kaizen proposals I've described were based on the objective of making our equipment and production methods more profitable. We will continue to refine our equipment systems so that they become an integral part of production.

Sharing Knowledge for Unlimited Improvement

(Mikkabi-chō Agricultural Cooperative)
by Masayuki Kaneko

Mikkabi-chō is a town of 16,000 people located in the western Shizuoka prefecture of Japan. It is surrounded by mountains on one side and a vast lake on the other. The town is famous as a scenic destination for tourists and also prides itself on a 200-year tradition of production of local specialties.

The membership of our cooperative association includes 2,800 families. We have 180 employees working in 3 divisions and 18 departments. The cooperative is involved in various business activities for the benefit of its members.

The cooperative sponsors five main activities for the benefit of its members:

- Cooperative financial services: The association provides protection for members in the form of life insurance as well as secure financing.
- Credit union: Financing is backed by savings of the members.
- Cooperative stores: These supply foodstuffs and other necessities, as well as fertilizers and animal fodder to improve the results of farming and livestock breeding.

- Sales and marketing: Our job is to make farming and livestock breeding more profitable.
- Planning and consulting: We provide assistance with economic management of farming and help improve the cultural life of the community.

Because we are an association of farmers, our members can use all of our establishments, such as various businesses, farmers' markets, fertilizer distribution centers, cooperative markets, home centers, parking lots, filling stations, and so on. Most of the farmers who live in the area join the association, which is why our facilities have a large number of users. These many businesses cover a wide range of activities.

I joined the cooperative in 1969, and until 1982 I worked as a car mechanic and maintenance worker. To give an example of the problems we faced, the hose that people used to wash their cars often got tangled. This was always annoying to the members who use the hose.

I wasn't sure what a proposal was, but I had an idea that we should find a way to wind up the hose on a reel, so I wrote that up as my first proposal. Everyone's daily work includes many such petty annoyances. Why tolerate them? There may be a better way to do things, one that increases productivity in addition to eliminating the problem.

Let me give you some practical examples of our improvements. In our automotive maintenance shop, when we confirmed that vehicle had been received for repairs, we put a description of the repair job in the place where the actual work was done. However, the descriptions were all written on the same kind of paper, so no one could tell who was to do what. And since there was no system for organizing these pages, they were tucked anywhere on the literature rack. This meant we had to go through all the papers one by one and put our stamps on the pages that applied to our jobs.

My improvement idea was to organize the sections on the literature rack according to the different types of service and to use different colors of paper for different kinds of repair jobs. Urgent jobs were stamped priority.

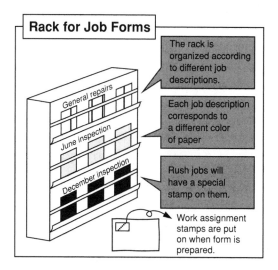

Rack for Job Forms

General repairs

June inspection

December inspection

The rack is organized according to different job descriptions.

Each job description corresponds to a different color of paper

Rush jobs will have a special stamp on them.

Work assignment stamps are put on when form is prepared.

Although the reviewer accepted my proposal, she wrote back, "We should examine whether we could improve it further by taking more concrete measures and by making it more economical." I was perplexed. What did she mean by "examine"? If it is always so much trouble, I decided, I am not going to write any more proposals.

At this point I remembered an old saying, "The knowledge that three people can share is boundless." If you contemplate a problem all alone, you may come up with a good idea. But when several people put their heads together, they are bound to come up with a clever plan.

With that in mind, one day I got together with some friends who were interested in making improvement proposals — Masao (M) from the home center, Kazuo (K) from the market department, and me, Masayuki (M), from the maintenance shop. That was the start of our small group, "MMK Planning."

We met together on a regular basis, with an agenda we had thought about. We decided which proposals each of us would formally submit and what methods we should use. Then followed an exchange of opinions on that topic.

Ideas sometimes come when you let your mind relax a bit. Once in February, I just couldn't think of any proposals. I went up to the top of the cooperative's meeting hall and gazed at the starry sky for a while. It was so beautiful. It looked as if the sky were filled with precious stones. Since my birthday was coming up, I wondered what the birthstone for February was. Then I got the idea to hold a monthly birthday party for all the members born that month. It could be a luncheon attended by the chairman of the association, and we could take pictures of the event. This would give people a sense that their membership was valuable to the association.

That idea became a proposal. The proposal was accepted, and the monthly birthday parties continue today.

Other improvements came from our realization that problems with purchasing should not be dealt with by the purchasing department alone, but also should be understood by every employee of the cooperative.

I am pleased to add that in 1982 we were awarded a prize for the largest number of proposals made by one group, and we also received the prize for individual proposals.

Not long after that, I was transferred to my present position in the consulting department. My job, in which I no longer work with cars but with people, has two main facets:

- Consulting related to general, economic, and farming activities of the members
- Advising the cooperative's leadership in its role in promoting structural change

In this capacity, I think constantly about the problems faced by the cooperative. I have to prepare plans that will meet the needs of a changing period. I am also able to experience first-hand the changes of the workplace.

For example, the cards we sent out to notify members about an upcoming meeting used to say only, "Do not forget to attend the meeting on X date at Y time and Z location." Under our new program, the cards looked very different. They were much more personal and polite, including a friendly greeting and an expression of our appreciation for their participation.

Last year the cooperative formed new committees for promoting proposals and giving them written reviews. The committees encourage members to participate in management activities, emphasizing creativity and ingenuity. One of our most important goals is to make proposal activities more enjoyable. To achieve this, we treat even small proposals and ideas with respect. For example, even when a proposal is not accepted, the committee's opinion is provided in writing to motivate and educate the proposal writers. We care about the professional development of our innovators. At first I did not know how to write proposals, but the feedback and group discussion helped me learn.

Proposals create motivation to participate in management, bring new energy to the workplace, and encourage study and self-improvement.

Our proposal activities reflect a commonsense approach to problems. The fact that every member of the cooperative participated in proposal activity clearly made our work there easier. Everyone has something to contribute. Our results can only improve if we continue to educate our members.

In the future we will do our best to motivate small group activities and to stimulate proposal activities on relevant topics, planning and review, goal setting, analysis of important factors, and theoretical explanations of measures and effects.

Kaizen Proposal Activity to Improve Printed Circuit Board Production

(Sony Kōda, Ltd.)
by Nagahito Iwamoto

My introduction to kaizen activities came soon after I was hired at Sony, during an orientation session that introduced us to the company's kaizen proposal system. At the time, I didn't fully understand what kaizen proposals were.

Assigned to a line for production of videotape recorders, I was so busy every day that I soon forgot all about kaizen proposals. One day the supervisor told me that I should submit at least one proposal a year, and urged me to think of something.

I had no idea what I should write about or what direction to look in. A senior employee sensed that I was agonizing over it and counseled, "If you have to rack your brain like that, you will end up with a proposal that will be difficult to implement." I took her words to heart and wrote my first proposal.

Sony Kōda is located in the Aichi prefecture of Japan. Founded in 1972, it employs 1,900 people to produce videotape recorders. I work in production section 3 (printed boards), where we fit printed circuits into circuit boards.

After a year and a half, I received an unexpected promotion to production line leader in the printed circuit board department. It was now my job to supervise other people.

At the time, things were not going well with that particular production line. In fact, it had suffered a series of failures. Moreover, the quality of products and productivity were poor.

The section manager spoke to me strongly about it. He told me to take a good look at the production line and come up with some improvements.

His assignment threw me into a state of panic. I was totally stymied about what to do.

I confessed to the section manager that I didn't understand what proposals were about or how to write them. His response was to ask, "Why not form a proposal group? With a group, you will have more opportunities to learn about proposals that could be useful for improving your production line."

When I took a good look at the proposals of others, I saw that most of them involved things that people had close contact with on the job. I realized that I could do things like that. Suddenly I felt more hopeful about the possibilities.

Finally I had my first major opportunity to get involved with a kaizen proposal. When the operator concentrated on inserting the parts on a board, he or she would sometimes forget to move the board off the conveyor. When this happened, the board kept moving and collided with the safety cover on the end of the belt, destroying the board and its components. The operator who made the mistake felt miserable about it and usually got a reprimand. Wasn't there a way to prevent the loss and the consequent damage to the operator's morale?

Thinking about it after hours, I had an idea. I was so excited about it that I stayed after work to implement it. The improvement was a warning mechanism that signaled to the operator when a board got within 60 cm of the safety cover. The operator was relieved to have a way to avoid the mistake.

This was my first real kaizen proposal. When I told the section manager about it, he said, "That's what I call kaizen! In the future, when you notice something that doesn't look right, write me a memo and let's improve it."

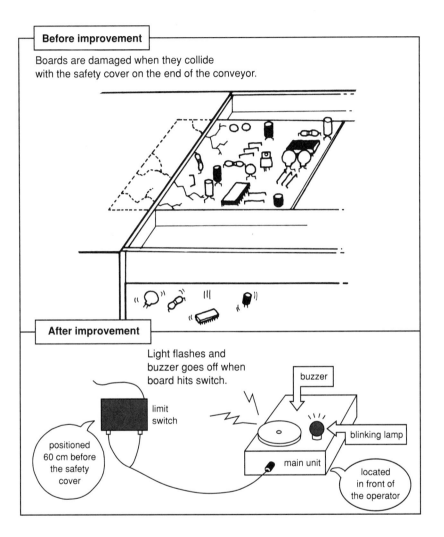

I began carrying notepads in my pockets so that I would not forget to write a memo if I saw something that needed improvement. I decided I would spend a half hour before bedtime formulating my improvements by writing them down on the proposal form. Soon, however, I noticed that I just wasn't getting results working on the ideas alone.

That is why I started explaining kaizen proposals to the other operators during the morning meeting. I asked them to please tell me about operations that were difficult to perform or things that didn't look right. Initially, I didn't get much of a response.

As I did the rounds of the production line, I listened to what each operator had to say. I was trying to instill the innovative spirit in each of them by reminding them that there was no room for compromise in their work and that there must be better ways to do things. Sometimes I asked them whether they thought there was anything strange in the operations they did. Usually, even if they did think that some operations made no sense, they were reluctant to talk about it. This informal attention opened them up a bit, however, and one week they made 150 proposals!

Thanks to this activity, both the productivity and the quality of the products on my line have improved.

For example, it used to be a big problem when we introduced new models; the boards required so many new operations. The problems increased once the models were on the production line. As I inspected the production line one day, I noticed that the biggest problems were in component soldering.

In an operation to attach small component "legs" to the board, the soldering iron wasn't hot enough to do the job. Our solution was to increase its capacity from 18 watts to 26 watts.

After we did this, we noticed another problem — the soldering iron wore out more quickly at these higher temperatures, creating a rounded cross-section on the tip that was not capable of heating both the leg and the board at the same time.

We tried using a narrow soldering finger, but this was not a good solution because the operation took too long. The soldering fingers available on the market were not suitable for this kind of operation. The only solution was to produce our own improved version of the soldering finger.

After trying many shapes, we found an angled tip that was most suitable for this particular soldering operation. But when we used that shape, the temperature of the soldering tip quickly dropped. Next we decided to use a blunt-tip soldering finger at a temperature generated by 55 watts. It had excellent heat efficiency but got so hot that the solder did not adhere to the material.

Finally, we returned to our idea of using the angled tip at 55 watts, and also adapted the jig that held the board so that it tilted at a 30-degree angle. This increased the surface area touched by the soldering iron so that it was hot enough to attach the leg components. With this setup, the operation is faster and we don't have to worry about poor quality anymore.

Solving New Model Production Problems

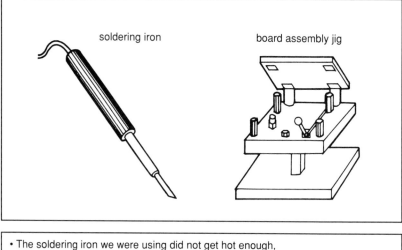

soldering iron

board assembly jig

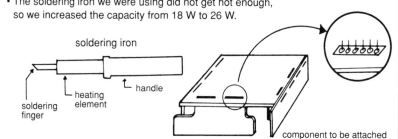

- The soldering iron we were using did not get hot enough, so we increased the capacity from 18 W to 26 W.

soldering iron

soldering finger

heating element

handle

component to be attached

The solution creates new problems:

As the soldering iron now reached higher temperatures, its tip was used up faster and quickly became rounded. When this happened, it no longer properly soldered the desired pattern because it could not heat the board adequately at the same time as it heated the leg.

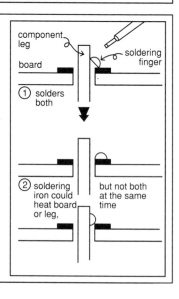

component leg

board

soldering finger

① solders both

② soldering iron could heat board or leg,

but not both at the same time

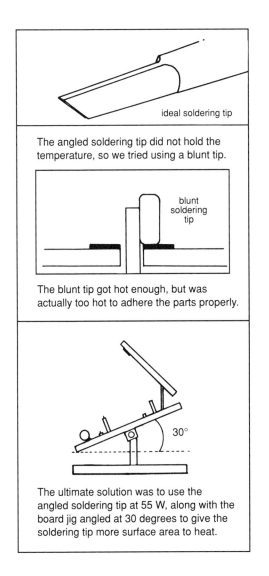

ideal soldering tip

The angled soldering tip did not hold the temperature, so we tried using a blunt tip.

blunt soldering tip

The blunt tip got hot enough, but was actually too hot to adhere the parts properly.

30°

The ultimate solution was to use the angled soldering tip at 55 W, along with the board jig angled at 30 degrees to give the soldering tip more surface area to heat.

Harmonious Improvement Through Kaizen Teian

(Toyota Motor Co.)
by Akihiko Hasegawa

I work at the general assembly plant of the Toyota Motor Company headquarters in Toyota City in Japan. The slogan in our plant is Kaizen Activity to Build an Intelligent Future Overflowing with Our Living Tradition. With this slogan in mind, we work hard day and night building cars to be number one in customer satisfaction.

At our plant, there is a spirit of cooperation between the assembly line and the improvement and maintenance section. Since I work in a department of the improvement and maintenance section, my responsibility is directly connected to the work on the assembly line.

We have many improvements that are good examples of the Toyota production system in our plant. Our plant's main kaizen objectives are lower costs, better quality, and safety on the production line.

When I joined the company in 1973, I was assigned to the section that was in charge of maintenance of accessories. Since I dreamed of becoming an engineer, I was thrilled that my job was directly related to the assembly line. This meant that I could be involved in mechanical designing, which was my passion.

At that time, however, maintenance work consisted mostly of making boxes and shelves to store nuts and bolts. We also had to make ramps for the painting plant and do other types of work usually done by blacksmiths. And when the assembly plant needed people, they asked us to come in and work on the line. I wondered if this was how engineers got started!

Every day they asked us to help out in some place or other, and on top of that, since we were from maintenance, they wanted us to make improvements for them. As a new employee, I lacked both the know-how and the technical skills to do this. I felt woefully inadequate having to ask senior employees to help me on a daily basis. As other new-hires and some of my friends left the company, I thought maybe it would be best if I left too.

My group leader came to talk to me about it. "Let me get this straight. You want to quit because the assembly plant always calls on you to help out and each time it's with a different line. Listen, your situation is not that bad, you know. In my time, I had to put in time all over the place — just name any part of the plant!"

When I asked the group leader for advice, he told me that in his opinion, I was gaining experience that would prove valuable in the future, although I didn't realize it. Some advice, I thought. This was a difficult time for me.

One day, the group leader came to me and said, "Listen, the floor of that line got dirty from the oil and it's hard to work there. Can you think of some improvement that would put an end to this?" I couldn't say a thing — my head was completely empty. There was not a single idea there.

"The most important thing," he told me, "is to take a good look at the place."

Later, I had another chance. A "railroad tie" is a block placed on top of the conveyor to mount frames on. The operator had to put them on the conveyor at the beginning of the line, and then take them off the conveyor one by one at the end of the line, when the same operation would begin again.

I knew this operation from personal experience because I had been asked to help out occasionally. I had hated that job because I always got dirty and my hands were full of splinters from the block.

After thinking about it for a while, I came up with the idea of mechanizing the tie-placing job. I developed a concept of the machine, then talked with managers and colleagues until we reached a workable solution. This became my first implemented proposal.

Two months later, my supervisor called me over to tell me that my proposal was awarded the prize for excellence! I was elated. Then my boss said, "By the way, Hasegawa, you used to submit one idea a month, and you haven't turned any in yet this month."

"Yes, well, you keep sending me to help out other people and I have no time to propose anything," I replied.

"You mean to tell me that you don't have any proposals because I am lending you out?" He wasn't too pleased with my perspective.

"I also had to make two guide bars because the bolts did not fit a machine at one of the places where I was helping out," I added. I was not completely useless at kaizen.

Then he said, "Your tie-setting machine broke down. Will you go over and lend them a hand?"

Kaizen is based on confronting the problems we face in the workplace. After that, I came to see my helping out in different places as practical on-the-job training.

However, when a person lacks the knowledge, technical skills, and other abilities that are increasingly required for kaizen, it is like hitting a brick wall. I knew I couldn't continue like that. I knew I needed to study and teach myself what I needed to know. Ultimately, through my studies, I obtained 15 different authorizations and licenses.

IMPROVEMENT EXAMPLES

I'd like to share some practical kaizen examples I was able to work out thanks to the skills I learned.

Toyota's engines travel on a transport chassis. We have 871 car models for eight different types of cars, and the number of engines used in those cars is even greater than that. We often have to stop and change the sling used to lift each engine off the chassis, and every time it slows down the line.

Our kaizen idea was to create a semirigid sling with various hooks that could be used to lift any type of engine. The hooks not needed for a particular engine were fastened out of the way with magnets. This new sling reduced the types of hoisting tools required from 21 to 4.

One production line made eight different models and had the largest number of different parts to be attached. Near the line, there were parts storage shelves for each model. Each shelf was wide, requiring the operator walk several paces. All this walking slowed down the whole process. What we needed was

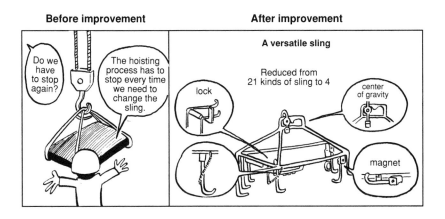

a method that would make it possible to quickly obtain the re-quired parts without all the walking.

I wondered if we could devise a unit that would hold the parts and do all the moving for us. I thought about my little tape player. Maybe we could use something like a cassette that would slide in and out, holding different parts for each model.

I talked to people who worked on that line right away. We put together a cassette-type storage unit for the parts. When you press the button to select the part for your model, the part comes out of the storage compartment in a cassette.

In 1974, Mr. Nakajima became the new technical specialist. Mr. Nakajima was always observing the way things were done at the plant and thinking about how to improve things through kaizen. We got a milling machine and a lathe to help us imple-ment automated kaizen ideas, such as a rotating frame for ex-change of engine chassis. Our kaizen activities became very vigorous.

As the number of proposals grew, the section leader asked one day if I had heard about the creativity award and whether we would like to compete for it. These prizes went to only 300 employees each year: 200 copper prizes, 60 silver prizes, and 40 gold prizes. We decided to give it a shot.

Before improvement

After improvement

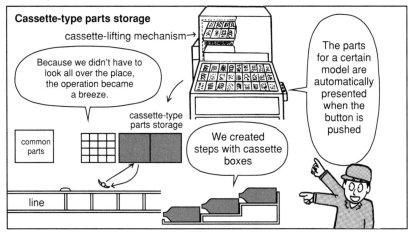

We began by keeping a diary of our kaizen improvements. We asked the section leader's advice on planning our proposals. His guidance helped us clearly describe the proposals and methods. That alone gave our proposal activity greater value.

When I received one of the prizes that year, it seemed to trigger a chain reaction, so that every year a number of members of my group received prizes. From 1981 to 1987, 11 people won kaizen proposal awards. Because our collective was so successful, we were awarded the Best Plant commendation at the end of 1984.

In 1986 I was promoted to group leader. Soon enough, I found that having to supervise other people was a big headache. The amount of work increased, and now I not only had to worry about my own work but also had to keep track of what other people were doing.

Busy as I was, the section leader kept asking me, "Something is wrong with that production line. Won't you give them a hand?" I didn't know what to do at first, but he wouldn't stop asking until I agreed to help.

I sat everyone down and said, "Let's put our heads together and see if we can come up with a good idea." But good advice is sometimes hard to take. It fast became clear that being a leader is like walking down a thorny road, and I was just taking my first steps on that road.

About that time, two senior employees were assigned to my group. Since they had worked on the production line for a long time, they surely knew the problem areas very well. Nevertheless, they didn't write any proposals. Their reluctance seemed to be related to their feelings about reporting to a younger person as their group leader. I wondered how to ease the antagonism that seemed to exist.

The idea I had was an overnight fishing trip on the ocean. I thought that getting together outside the work environment might ease some tensions and open up communication between the senior employees and myself.

During this trip, unfortunately, one of the veterans and I both got terribly seasick. It was a great equalizer. The other senior employee felt bad for me and helped me get through it. In spite of our misfortune, or perhaps because of it, the relations between the people working in my group became less tense.

One day soon afterward, one of the senior workers approached me on the work floor. "Don't you think it would be a good idea if we had a machine that would produce six nuts at a time?" he asked. "I've been thinking about how to do that." I was amazed — this was the first time he had suggested anything! He was right: the work would be much easier if we had such a machine. I encouraged him to pursue the idea. Through trial and error, the worker improved his productivity by 80 percent. The young worker was obviously flattered.

Finally the day came when the machine was ready to try. Sure enough, the nuts came out of the machine in the desired quantity. We installed it in the shop right away. I was so impressed that I could not find the right words to praise them.

The other senior employee was not idle during this time. He completed a revolving hoisting hook that saved us money. Our workshop was brimming with the spirit of cooperation and competition, which provided new energy for our work. As a result, our proposal activity became more intensive and we reached an even higher level.

Since we have a great number of different lines, it is difficult to determine correctly the causes of minor problems. For that reason, we began using a video camera. The video image gave us an overall view of the situation and of the causes of problems, which helped us to achieve further progress and even greater improvement. Video also facilitated discussion by making it possible for all the employees to participate.

In conclusion, let me emphasize that a spirit of harmony arises in a workplace where the kaizen movement is thriving. This spirit fuels the "Three Cs": creativity, challenge, and courage.

Postscript

The Japan Human Relations Association prepares kaizen teian programs in response to specific requests from various organizations for study sessions and lectures. Different companies have different needs, and no single type of study session proves to be the most effective one.

Nevertheless, it is important to pursue periodic growth and development of kaizen proposal activities. We need to approach the issue on the basis of an analysis of why proposal activity lapses or why people slip back into old habits.

It is indispensable to ask what the objectives of the kaizen movement are in your company. You also need to ask what is the best way to promote the activities and what form they should take.

The *Kaizen Teian* book series is a basic interpretation of how to study such issues. Volume 1, *Developing Systems for Continuous Improvement through Employee Suggestions*, explains the mechanism of improvement proposals and strategies for making the mechanism work. This book (Volume 2 of the series) explains the principles of kaizen and offers guidelines for a kaizen teian system.

189

We strongly recommend that these books be studied by managers and supervisors, kaizen proposal activity administrators and promotors, and other workplace leaders. The reason for that is simple. Promotion of proposals as a form of on-the-job training requires a common understanding of the intricate relationships between all employees. If this understanding is lacking, no amount of persuasion and entreaties to "give us some proposals" will amount to anything.

The principles put forward in this book are examples of actual improvement proposals. We are indebted to the organizations that provided us with these examples. Kaizen teian activity is built on the promise that knowledge of how to improve the workplace should come from the workplace itself. We deeply appreciate the cooperation of the people who offered us this material.

The main points of this book can be expressed as follows:

- Ideas about work are born out of work.
- Ideas about a particular area can be born only in that area.

That is why we say in this book that only people who do a particular job can come up with the appropriate way to improve it. We advocate implementing ideas that spring from the workplace itself, even if this can be done only little by little at first. This is the essence of kaizen teian activity and its reason for existing. If those ideas exist, it means that they can be used, and therein lies their value.

Index

Books from Productivity Press

Productivity Press publishes books that empower individuals and companies to achieve excellence in quality, productivity, and the creative involvement of all employees. Through steadfast efforts to support the vision and strategy of continuous improvement, Productivity Press delivers today's leading-edge tools and techniques gathered directly from industry leaders around the world. Call toll-free (800) 394-6868 for our free catalog.

The Improvement Engine
Creativity and Innovation Through Employee Involvement—The Kaizen Teian System
JHRA (ed.)

The Improvement Engine offers the most all inclusive information available today on this proven method for increasing employee involvement. Kaizen Teian is a technique developed in Japan for encouraging employees to constantly look for and make improvement suggestions. This book explores the subtleties between designing a moderately successful program and a highly successful one and includes a host of tools, techniques, and case studies.
ISBN 1-56327-010-2 / 155 pages / $40.00 / Order IMPENG-B204

Building a Shared Vision
A Leader's Guide to Aligning the Organization
C. Patrick Lewis

This exciting new book presents a step-by-step method for developing your organizational vision. It teaches how to build and maintain a shared vision directed from the top down, but encompassing the views of all the members and stakeholders, and understanding the competitive environment of the organization. Like *Corporate Diagnosis*, this books describes in detail one of the necessary first steps from *Implementing a Lean Management System:* visioning.
ISBN 1-56327-163-X / 150 pages / $45.00 / Order VISION-B204

Secrets of a Successful Employee Recognition System
Daniel C. Boyle

As the human resource manager of a failing manufacturing plant, Dan Boyle was desperate to find a way to motivate employees and break down the barrier between management and the union. He came up with a simple idea—say thank you to your employees for doing their job. In *Secrets to a Successful Employee Recognition System,* Boyle outlines how to begin and run a 100 Club program. Filled with case studies and detailed guidelines, this book underscores the power behind thanking your employees for a job well done.
ISBN 1-56327-083-8 / 250 pages / $25.00 / Order SECRET-B204

Productivity Press, Dept. BK, P.O. Box 13390, Portland, OR 97213-0390
Telephone: 1-800-394-6868   Fax: 1-800-394-6286

20 Keys to Workplace Improvement *(Revised)*
Iwao Kobayashi

The 20 Keys system does more than just bring together twenty of the world's top manufacturing improvement approaches—it integrates these individual methods into a closely interrelated system for revolutionizing every aspect of your manufacturing organization. This revised edition of Kobayashi's best-seller amplifies the synergistic power of raising the levels of all these critical areas simultaneously. The new edition presents upgraded criteria for the five-level scoring system in most of the 20 Keys, supporting your progress toward becoming not only best in your industry but best in the world. New material and an updated layout throughout assist managers in implementing this comprehensive approach. In addition, valuable case studies describe how Morioka Seiko (Japan) advanced in Key 18 (use of microprocessors) and how Windfall Products (Pennsylvania) adapted the 20 Keys to its situation with good results.
ISBN 1-56327-109-5/ est 275 pages / $50.00 / Order 20KREV-B204

Feedback Toolkit
16 Tools for Better Communication in the Workplace
Rick Maurer

In companies striving to reduce hierarchy and foster trust and responsible participation, good person-to-person feedback can be as important as sophisticated computer technology in enabling effective teamwork. Feedback is an important map of your situation, a way to tell whether you are "on or off track." Used well, feedback can motivate people to their highest level of performance. Despite its significance, this level of information sharing makes most managers uncomfortable. *Feedback Toolkit* addresses this natural hesitation with an easy-to-grasp 6-step framework and 16 practical and creative approaches for giving and receiving feedback with individuals and groups. Maurer's reality-tested methods in *Feedback Toolkit* are indispensable equipment for managers and teams in every organization.
ISBN 1-56327-056-0 / 109 pages / $12.00 / Order FEED-B204

Building Organizational Fitness
Management Methodology for Transformation and Strategic Advantage
Ryuji Fukuda

The most urgent task for companies today is to take a hard look at the future. To remain competitive, management must nurture a strong capability for self-development and a strong corporate culture, both of which form part of the foundation for improvement. But simply understanding management techniques doesn't mean you know how to use them. You need the tools and technologies for implementation. In *Building Organizational Fitness*, Fukuda extends the power of his managerial engineering methodology into the context of the top management strategic planning role.
ISBN 1-56327-144-3 / 250 pages / $65.00 / Order BFIT-B204

Productivity Press, Dept. BK, P.O. Box 13390, Portland, OR 97213-0390
Telephone: 1-800-394-6868   Fax: 1-800-394-6286

Corporate Diagnosis
Setting the Global Standard for Excellence
Thomas L. Jackson with Constance E. Dyer

All too often, strategic planning neglects an essential first step and final step-diagnosis of the organization's current state. What's required is a systematic review of the critical factors in organizational learning and growth, factors that require monitoring, measurement, and management to ensure that your company competes successfully. This executive workbook provides a step-by-step method for diagnosing an organization's strategic health and measuring its overall competitiveness against world class standards. With checklists, charts, and detailed explanations, *Corporate Diagnosis* is a practical instruction manual. The pillars of Jackson's diagnostic system are strategy, structure, and capability. Detailed diagnostic questions in each area are provided as guidelines for developing your own self-assessment survey.

ISBN 1-56327-086-2 / 115 pages / $65.00 / Order CDIAG-B204

Do it Right the Second Time
Benchmarking Best Practices in the Quality Change Process
Peter Merrill

Is your organization looking back on its quality process and saying "it failed"? Are you concerned that TQM is just another fad, only to be replaced by the next improvement movement? Don't jump ship just yet. Everyone experiences failures in their quality improvement process. Successful organizations are different because they learn from their failure: They do it right the second time. In this plain-speaking, easy-to-read book, Peter Merrill helps companies take what they learned from their first attempts at implementing a quality program, rethink the plan, and move forward. He takes you sequentially through the activities required to lead a lasting change from vision to final realization. Each brief chapter covers a specific topic in a framework which leads you directly to the issues that concern your organization.

ISBN 1-56327-175-3 / 225 pages / $27.00 / Order RSEC-B204

The Hunters and the Hunted
A Non-Linear Solution for Reengineering the Workplace
James B. Swartz

Our competitive environment changes rapidly. If you want to survive, you have to stay on top of those changes. Otherwise, you become prey to your competitors. Hunters continuously change and learn; anyone who doesn't becomes the hunted and sooner or later will be devoured. This unusual non-fiction novel provides a veritable crash course in continuous transformation. It offers lessons from real-life companies and introduces many industrial gurus as characters. *The Hunters and the Hunted* doesn't simply tell you how to change; it puts you inside the change process itself.

ISBN 1-56327-043-9 / 564 pages / $45.00 / Order HUNT-B204

Productivity Press, Dept. BK, P.O. Box 13390, Portland, OR 97213-0390
Telephone: 1-800-394-6868   Fax: 1-800-394-6286

Thoughtware
Change the Thinking and the Organization Will Change Itself
J. Philip Kirby & D.H. Hughes

In order to facilitate true change in an organization, its thinking patterns need to be the first thing to change. Your employees need more than empowerment. They need to move from doing their jobs to doing whatever is needed for the good of the entire organization. Thoughtware is the underlying platform on which every organization operates, the set of assumptions upon which the organization is structured. When you understand and change thoughtware, the tools and techniques of continuous improvement become incredibly powerful.
ISBN 1-56327-106-0 / 200 pages / $35.00 / Order THOUG-B204

Caught in the Middle
A Leadership Guide for Partnership in the Workplace
Rick Maurer

Managers today are caught between old skills and new expectations. You're expected not only to improve quality and services, but also to get staff more involved. This stimulating book provides the inspiration and know-how to achieve these goals as it brings to light the rewards of establishing a real partnership with your staff. Includes self-assessment questionnaires.
ISBN 1-56327-004-8 / 258 pages / $30.00 / Order CAUGHT-B204

Fast Focus on TQM
A Concise Guide to Companywide Learning
Derm Barrett

Finally, here's one source for all your TQM questions. Compiled in this concise, easy-to-read handbook are definitions and detailed explanations of over 160 key terms used in TQM. Organized in a simple alphabetical glossary form, the book can be used either as a primer for anyone being introduced to TQM or as a complete reference guide. It helps to align teams, departments, or entire organizations in a common understanding and use of TQM terminology. For anyone entering or currently involved in TQM, this is one resource you must have.
ISBN 1-56327-049-8 / 186 pages / $20.00 / Order FAST-B204

The Idea Book
Improvement Through TEI (Total Employee Involvement)
Japan Human Relations Association

At last, a book showing how to create Total Employee Involvement (TEI) and get hundreds of ideas from each employee every year to improve every aspect of your organization. Gathering improvement ideas from your entire workforce is a must for global competitiveness. *The Idea Book,* heavily illustrated, is a hands-on teaching tool for workers and supervisors to refer to again and again. Perfect for study groups, too.
ISBN 0-915299-22-4 / 232 pages / $55.00 / Order IDEA-B204

Productivity Press, Dept. BK, P.O. Box 13390, Portland, OR 97213-0390
Telephone: 1-800-394-6868   Fax: 1-800-394-6286

Learning Organizations
Developing Cultures for Tomorrow's Workplace
Sarita Chawla and John Renesch, Editors

The ability to learn faster than your competition may be the only sustainable competitive advantage! A learning organization is one where people continually expand their capacity to create results they truly desire, where new and expansive patterns of thinking are nurtured, where collective aspiration is set free, and where people are continually learning how to learn together. This compilation of 34 powerful essays, written by recognized experts world-wide, is rich in concept and theory as well as application and example. An inspiring followup to Peter Senge's ground-breaking best-seller *The Fifth Discipline,* these essays are grouped in four sections that address all aspects of learning organizations: the guiding ideas behind systems thinking; the theories, methods, and processes for creating a learning organization; the infrastructure of the learning model; and arenas of practice.
ISBN 1-56327-110-9 / 575 pages / $35.00 / Order LEARN-B204

Implementing a Lean Management System
Thomas L. Jackson with Karen R. Jones

Does your company think and act ahead of technological change, ahead of the customer, and ahead of the competition? Thinking strategically requires a company to face these questions with a clear future image of itself. *Implementing a Lean Management System* lays out a comprehensive management system for aligning the firm's vision of the future with market realities. Based on hoshin management, the Japanese strategic planning method used by top managers for driving TQM throughout an organization, Lean Management is about deploying vision, strategy, and policy to all levels of daily activity. It is an eminently practical methodology emerging out of the implementation of continuous improvement methods and employee involvement. The key tools of this book build on multiskilling, the knowledge of the worker, and an understanding of the role of the new lean manufacturer.
ISBN 1-56327-085-4 / 182 pages / $65.00 / Order ILMS-B204

Putting Performance Measurement to Work
Building focus and Sustaining Improvement
(Action Learning software application)
Learner First with Brian H. Maskell

For optimal results in your improvement efforts, the introduction of new performance measures needs to go hand in hand with the introduction of new manufacturing techniques. You choose what area of improvement to focus on, determine the improvement, determine the measures, and put them in place. Then you move to the next area to be improved and you do the same thing. Easy, right? This software application will teach you, coach you, help you determine then achieve your goals and lead you to success.
ISBN 1-56327-171-0 /Manual 250 pages / $495.00 / Order PERFSW-B204

Productivity Press, Dept. BK, P.O. Box 13390, Portland, OR 97213-0390
Telephone: 1-800-394-6868   Fax: 1-800-394-6286

TO ORDER: Write, phone, or fax Productivity Press, Dept. BK, P.O. Box 13390, Portland, OR 97213-0390, phone 1-800-394-6868, fax 1-800-394-6286. Outside the U.S. phone (503) 235-0600; fax (503) 235-0909. Send check or charge to your credit card (American Express, Visa, MasterCard accepted).

U.S. ORDERS: Add $5 shipping for first book, $2 each additional for UPS surface delivery. Add $5 for each AV program containing 1 or 2 tapes; add $12 for each AV program containing 3 or more tapes. We offer attractive quantity discounts for bulk purchases of individual titles; call for more information.

ORDER BY E-MAIL: Order 24 hours a day from anywhere in the world. Use either address:
To order: service@ppress.com
To view the online catalog and/or order: http://www.ppress.com/

QUANTITY DISCOUNTS: For information on quantity discounts, please contact our sales department.

INTERNATIONAL ORDERS: Write, phone, or fax for quote and indicate shipping method desired. For international callers, telephone number is 503-235-0600 and fax number is 503-235-0909. Prepayment in U.S. dollars must accompany your order (checks must be drawn on U.S. banks). When quote is returned with payment, your order will be shipped promptly by the method requested.

NOTE: Prices are in U.S. dollars and are subject to change without notice.

About the Shopfloor Series

Put powerful and proven improvement tools in the hands of your entire workforce!

Progressive shopfloor improvement techniques are imperative for manufacturers who want to stay competitive and to achieve world class excellence. And it's the comprehensive education of all shopfloor workers that ensures full participation and success when implementing new programs. The Shopfloor Series books make practical information accessible to everyone by presenting major concepts and tools in simple, clear language and at a reading level that has been adjusted for operators by skilled instructional designers. One main idea is presented every two to four pages so that the book can be picked up and put down easily. Each chapter begins with an overview and ends with a summary section. Helpful illustrations are used throughout.

Books currently in the Shopfloor Series include:

5S FOR OPERATORS
5 Pillars of the Visual Workplace
The Productivity Press Development Team
ISBN 1-56327-123-0 / incl. application questions / 133 pages
Order 5SOP-B204 / $25.00

QUICK CHANGEOVER FOR OPERATORS
The SMED System
The Productivity Press Development Team
ISBN 1-56327-125-7 / incl. application questions / 93 pages
Order QCOOP-B204 / $25.00

MISTAKE-PROOFING FOR OPERATORS
The Productivity Press Development Team
ISBN 1-56327-127-3 / 93 pages
Order ZQCOP-B204 / $25.00

TPM FOR SUPERVISORS
The Productivity Press Development Team
ISBN 1-56327-161-3 / 96 pages
Order TPMSUP-B204 / $25.00

TPM TEAM GUIDE
Kunio Shirose
ISBN 1-56327-079-X / 175 pages
Order TGUIDE-B204 / $25.00

TPM FOR EVERY OPERATOR
Japan Institute of Plant Maintenance
ISBN 1-56327-080-3 / 136 pages
Order TPMEO-B204 / $25.00

Productivity Press, Dept. BK, P.O. Box 13390, Portland, OR 97213-0390
Telephone: 1-800-394-6868   Fax: 1-800-394-6286

Continue Your Learning with In-House Training and Consulting from the Productivity Consulting Group

Consulting Services

For over a decade, an expansive client base continues to recommend the Productivity Consulting Group (PCG) to colleagues eager to accelerate their improvement efforts. We have established a lasting improvement process with companies from various industries, including textiles, printing and packaging, chemicals, and heavy equipment.

Assignments vary from results-driven trainings on the tools of Lean Production, to broad total company conversion projects dealing with strategic intent through organization design/redesign. Tailoring our methodology to accommodate site-specific organizational and performance considerations is a real strength of the Productivity Consulting Group.

Educational Resources

Our products and services are leading-edge, and have been used by most every company in the Fortune 500 and beyond. Topics include: Quick Changeover, Visual Workplace, Lean Production Systems, Total Productive Maintenance, and Mistake-Proofing.

We offer the following opportunities to enhance your improvement efforts: National Conferences, Training Events, Plant Tours, Industrial Study Missions, Master Series Workshops, and Newsletters.

Call the Productivity Consulting Group and learn how we can provide consulting services and educational resources customized to fit your changing needs.

Telephone: 1-800-966-5423 (U.S. only) or 1-203-846-3777
Fax: 1-203-846-6883

Productivity Press, Dept. BK, P.O. Box 13390, Portland, OR 97213-0390
Telephone: 1-800-394-6868   Fax: 1-800-394-6286